THE LITTLE RED BOOK OF

BASEBALL WISDOM

THE LITTLE RED BOOK OF
BASEBALL WISDOM

Edited by Wayne Stewart
Foreword by Roger Kahn

Skyhorse Publishing

Skyhorse Publishing books may be purchased in bulk at special discounts for sales promotion, corporate gifts, fund-raising, or educational purposes. Special editions can also be created to specifications. For details, contact the Special Sales Department, Skyhorse Publishing, 307 West 36th Street, 11th Floor, New York, NY 10018 or info@skyhorsepublishing.com. www.skyhorsepublishing.com

Skyhorse® and Skyhorse Publishing® are registered trademarks of Skyhorse Publishing, Inc.®, a Delaware corporation.

10 9 8 7 6 5 4 3 2 1

Library of Congress Cataloging-in-Publication Data is available on file.

ISBN: 978-1-61608-718-0

Printed in China

Contents

Introduction

Admittedly, this book contains some quotations that are apocryphal and/or spurious; some are certainly contrived, manufactured. Take, for instance, one of the many lines Yogi Berra supposedly said: "I didn't really say everything I said." Pedro Guerrero's take was slightly different when he commented, "Sometimes they write what I say and not what I mean." The bottom line is as simple as the cliché, "Don't believe everything you read."

Often, for example, once a quotation gets in circulation, it becomes accepted as the truth, whether the words were actually jotted down by, say, a ghostwriter, entirely fabricated by a reporter (said to be the case with "Say it ain't so, Joe."), or perhaps actually spoken by the subject then altered (consider the line "Nice guys finish last," discussed later).

Let's face it, baseball is notorious for building up legends, for putting words in players' mouths, and for embellishing both words and events. Who, for instance, could seriously believe that Willie Mays came up with such a line as "Baseball is a game, yes. It is also business. But what it most truly is is disguised combat. For all its gentility, its almost leisurely pace, baseball is violence under wraps." Gentility?! The word "gentility" from the "Say Hey Kid"? Forget about it.

This is the same Willie Mays who had Charles Einstein ghost write his biography, *My Life In and Out of Baseball,* yet a short time after working with Einstein, forgot his name. According to Bert Sugar's *Rain Delays,* at the end of the 1965 season when Einstein gave his subject a follow-up call, after having taken notes with Mays throughout the season and after having identified himself over the phone, Mays said, "Charley who?" When Einstein prompted, "You know, Charley Einstein, the fellow who is doing the book with you," Mays paused, then asked, "What book?"

It's not at all surprising either that some bursting-with-flavor quotes such as the great line about Mays's glove being where triples "go to die" is listed in various sources as having been spoken by Vin Scully, Fresco Thompson, and Jim Murray. Sometimes it's impossible to trace a great quotation to its true origin. In any event, baseball is richer for such classic comments, regardless of whoever first uttered them. Further, the vast majority of the quotes herein are right on the money regarding their legitimacy, their origin, and their purpose.

Therefore, nitpicking aside, here are some of the funniest, wittiest, most poignant, most incisive, and most revelatory words ever written or spoken about the game of baseball.

—*Wayne Stewart*
Lorain, Ohio

Foreword: The Talkers' Game

In his thoughtful and amiable work *Diamond Classics: The 100 Best Baseball Books Ever Published,* Mike Shannon, the author-editor, describes baseball as "the writers' game." Within his 455 pages, Shannon underscores his point with comment on such worthies as Ring Lardner, James T. Farrell, Mark Harris, Bernard Malamud, Eliot Asinof, and George Plimpton, who could be quite good when he stopped focusing on himself. Shelves today variously bulge and sag under an increasing burden from ostensibly literary baseball anthologies.

Why does baseball write so well, probably better than any other sport? Here are some factors:

Tradition. The major leagues trace to the nineteenth century. One of my own favorite baseball books, Christy Mathewson's *Pitching in a Pinch,* appeared in 1912. In a reasonably literate society such as ours, books build on one another.

Leisurely pace. A good ball game may last three hours, but no more than fifteen minutes is hard action. The rest of the time may be commercial space to the networks, but in the hands of a skillful author, it builds suspense.

Outsized characters. Mathewson, Ty Cobb, Babe Ruth, Leo Durocher, Joe DiMaggio, Jackie Robinson, Willie Mays. If an author can't write well about people like that, perhaps he had better peddle his keyboard and go into another field, say prawn diving.

Those, I suggest, are some reasons that baseball "writes." But my point here, and the point of this volume, is verbal. Baseball also "talks." No other sport comes close to matching baseball in jabber, prattle, impudence, abuse, wit, and sometimes even wisdom. Consider the folk who chatter in pages that follow:

Hank Aaron, a man with a bat.
Joe DiMaggio, as sure with one-liners as he was in center field.
Bart Giamatti, a commissioner with a PhD.
Shoeless Joe Jackson, eloquent in disgrace.
Mickey Mantle, funny if not always printable.
Walter O'Malley, who drove a spike through Brooklyn's heart.
Branch Rickey, baseball's Winston Churchill.
Damon Runyon, a nasty sort, but one of the most gifted sportswriters ever.
Red Smith, a genial sort, and one of the most gifted sportswriters ever.
Ted Williams, hit hard, lived hard, talked hard.
Dick Young, the prince (if such there be) of tabloid baseball writers.

Listening to many of these people has been one of the pleasures of my several years. Since I believe that the words define the man, I've always taken pains to quote people accurately and this has created a number of perplexing situations. The most annoying is the Misquote Syndrome. That appears when someone has made a remark that gets into print and lets loose swarms of controversy.

Caught in the furor, more than one baseball person has fallen back on what is for our purposes the big lie. "I never said that. Never even talked to the guy." A man who stood by quotes better than anyone else I encountered was Jackie Robinson. If a comment turned out to be ill-considered, Robinson might remark, "Maybe I shouldn't have said that, but I guess I did." Once Robinson said something, he stood by it. The worst on this issue of integrity? I don't want to be cruel, so no names here. Just initials. Pete Rose, the man whose word is worth its weight in fertilizer.

Sometimes an eager magazine editor calls and says he or she understands that bench-jockeying is pretty funny stuff and would I write an article about it. Yes and no. For years most bench jockeying was either sexual or ethnic. During the 1934 World Series, Hank Greenberg told me, Dizzy Dean kept shouting at him, "Hey, Moe!" (Dean shouted from a distance. Greenberg was a large, powerful man.) Thus rattled, Greenberg batted .321 across the seven games. The sexual stuff has usually been primitive. "Hey, I was out with yer wife last night and she ain't so hot, either." Not uproarious, but what were you expecting, Groucho Marx? I've heard one or two very funny sexual wisecracks boiling out of dugouts, but each gets a triple-X rating, hardly fit for mainstream magazines. Since the ethnic stuff is offensive, and most of the sexual cracks are fits for adolescent locker rooms, if anywhere, I don't think bench jockeying offers a basis for a magazine story.

Some baseball quotes are so venerable, they can only be attributed to that notable source, A. Non. Who first yelled at a failing batter, "You swing like a rusty gate"? Who first shouted about a faltering pitcher, "Take him out"? (That cry, Christy Mathewson said, bothered him more than any other.) How many generations ago did a hitter foul a pitch into a foot and hop about, prompting bench jockeys to bark, "Arf, arf"? Or shout, "Hey, getcha hot dogs"? We don't know. We do know that this kind of noise is part of the game.

In this volume, Wayne Stewart has undertaken the formidable task of preparing a baseball equivalent to *Bartlett's Familiar Quotations*. He has obviously worked with great energy, taste, and passion for the sport. Perfect? There is no perfect book. I would have added to Stewart's source material two defunct New York newspapers, the *World* and the *Herald Tribune*. Each is a trove of baseball writing gold. To his list of magazines I would add the late *Saturday Evening Post,* which first published Ring Lardner's 1916 classic, *You Know Me, Al.*

But these are minor reservations about a wonderful piece of work. Besides, they may encourage Mr. Stewart to proceed with future editions. He has my best, and I hope his eyesight holds.

—Roger Kahn
Stone Ridge, New York

PART ONE

The Classic Quotes

For the purposes of this chapter, the definition of "classic" is a bit elastic, expanded somewhat, to be sure. Dictionaries consider something to be a classic if it serves as a standard of excellence and has survived the test of time, but another definition is "historically noteworthy, of special note." Therefore, while the Joe Judge line about the Murderers' Row 1927 New York Yankees not merely beating opponents but also breaking teams' hearts, may not be one that is a standard nor one that the casual baseball fan might recognize, it is most certainly highly interesting, incisive, and worthy of note. Likewise, as is the case with ESPN's term "instant classic," some of the gems in this chapter are young but seem certain to ultimately pass the "test" of time.

Other quotes in this chapter are irrefutable baseball classics such as the words a dying Lou Gehrig spoke: "Fans, for the past two weeks you have been reading about what a bad break I got. Yet today I consider myself to be the luckiest man on the face of the earth."

While a scant handful of men included here are not the ones that are instantly recognizable, or usually associated with baseball, they are included, nevertheless, for their quotation contribution to the game of baseball. After all, this chapter not only includes the words of two National and one American League presidents, but also of United States president Calvin Coolidge juxtaposed with the words of men such as legendary baseball wordsmiths Yogi Berra, Casey Stengel, and Dizzy Dean. Toss into this odd mix comedian Joe E. Lewis, publisher William Feather, and Harry M. Stevens, the man who first conceived of the hot dog on a bun.

Further, some lines are so old the precise origin of the quotation has been lost or muddled through the passage of time. No one is positive, for example, who first uttered the words "Take two and hit to right," or "God takes care of little children and catchers." However, we do know that those words have lived throughout the annals of baseball.

Sometimes, too, as mentioned in the foreword, a great line has been attributed to more than one person. No matter, these classic lines can cause one to chuckle, to ruminate, and possibly even to consider the game in a new light.

• • •

The Classic Quotes

"Baseball is too much of a sport to be called a business and too much of a business to be called a sport."
—CUBS OWNER PHIL WRIGLEY

• • •

"You can't steal first."
—OLD BASEBALL ADAGE, SUPPOSEDLY FIRST SAID BY A MANAGER WHO APPARENTLY WASN'T FEARFUL OF EDDIE MAYO'S FOOT SPEED

• • •

"It's a great day for a ballgame; let's play two!"
—ENTHUSIASTIC CUBS STAR ERNIE BANKS

• • •

"A life is not important except in the impact it has on other lives."
—DODGERS STANDOUT JACKIE ROBINSON

• • •

"The trades you don't make are your best ones."
—ATTRIBUTED TO BASEBALL EXECUTIVE BRANCH RICKEY, ALSO ATTRIBUTED TO TEAM OWNER BILL VEECK

• • •

"Pitching is 75 percent of baseball."
—CONNIE MACK, OWNER AND MANAGER OF THE PHILADELPHIA A'S (SOMETIMES LISTED AS 80 PERCENT)

• • •

"What you see here—what you hear here—let it stay here— when you leave here."
—SAYING FOUND ON SIGNS POSTED IN TEAMS' CLUBHOUSES

• • •

"I felt nothing. Nothing."
—HALL OF FAMER TED WILLIAMS, WHEN ASKED WHAT HE FELT UPON HITTING HIS FINAL HOMER IN HIS LAST BIG LEAGUE TRIP TO THE PLATE

• • •

"Luck is the residue of design."
—BASEBALL EXECUTIVE BRANCH RICKEY

• • •

"Records are made to be broken."
—ATTRIBUTED TO MANY

• • •

"Baseball is the champ of them all. Like somebody said, the pay is short and the hours are good."
—CATCHER YOGI BERRA

• • •

"Oh, those bases on balls."
—BELIEVED TO HAVE FIRST BEEN UTTERED BY MANAGER GEORGE STALLINGS

• • •

"Say it ain't so, Joe. Say it ain't so."
—APOCRYPHAL LINE SAID TO BE UTTERED BY A YOUNG BOY TO "SHOELESS" JOE JACKSON UPON LEARNING THE 1919 WORLD SERIES HAD BEEN FIXED AND THAT JACKSON TOOK PART IN THE SCHEME; JACKSON WAS SAID TO HAVE REPLIED, "YES, KID, I'M AFRAID IT IS." ORIGINALLY FROM THE CHICAGO *HERALD AND EXAMINER*, SEPTEMBER 30, 1920, AND QUOTED IN *EIGHT MEN OUT* BY ELIOT ASINOF

• • •

"A good umpire is the umpire you don't even notice."
—AMERICAN LEAGUE PRESIDENT BAN JOHNSON

• • •

"If you don't play to win, why keep score?"
—PIRATES PITCHER VERNON LAW

• • •

"You can't win 'em all."
—ATTRIBUTED ORIGINALLY TO A'S MANAGER CONNIE MACK DURING AN ABYSMAL SEASON FOR HIS CLUB

• • •

"The other clubs would do better to stop worrying about breaking up the Yankees and start worrying about catching up to the Yankees."
—NEW YORK YANKEES OWNER JACOB RUPPERT

• • •

"It only takes one."
—TRADITIONAL BASEBALL TIP

• • •

"It ain't over til it's over."
—YANKEES GREAT YOGI BERRA

• • •

"My epitaph is inescapable. It will read: 'He sent a midget up to bat.'"
—COLORFUL TEAM OWNER BILL VEECK

• • •

"You lead by example."
—FORMER PLAYER AND MANAGER ALVIN DARK

• • •

"It ain't braggin' if you can do it."
—BRASH PITCHER DIZZY DEAN

• • •

"You can usually tell who's not going to make it. But when a scout tells you a player 'can't miss,' don't listen."
—PAUL RICHARDS AS A SCOUT

• • •

"I got to be first—all the time."
—THE HIGHLY DRIVEN TY COBB

• • •

"You don't save a pitcher for tomorrow. Tomorrow it may rain."
—MANAGER LEO DUROCHER

• • •

"An arm will rust out before it wears out."
—OLD BASEBALL ADAGE

• • •

"They [the 1927 Yankees] don't just beat you, they break your heart."
—SENATORS FIRST BASEMAN JOE JUDGE

• • •

"Don't send out your laundry."
—COMMON SPRING TRAINING WARNING TO MARGINAL PLAYERS SOON TO BE SENT PACKING TO THE MINORS OR CUT

• • •

"You measure the value of a ballplayer on how many fannies he puts in the seats."
—YANKEES OWNER GEORGE STEINBRENNER

• • •

"The road will make a bum out of the best of them."
—SPORTSWRITER HAROLD ROSENTHAL

• • •

"All I want out of life is that when I walk down the street, folks will say, 'There goes the greatest hitter who ever lived.'"
—BOSTON SUPERSTAR TED WILLIAMS

• • •

"If he'd just tip his cap once, he could be elected Mayor of Boston in five minutes."
—HALL OF FAMER EDDIE COLLINS ON TED WILLIAMS

• • •

"There is no defense against the walk."
—TRADITIONAL ADVICE TO PITCHERS

• • •

"You can't tell the players without a scorecard."
—HARRY M. STEVENS, THE MAN GIVEN CREDIT FOR THE INVENTION OF THE SCORECARD AND THE HOT DOG ON A ROLL

• • •

"I can think of three managers who weren't fired. John McGraw of the Giants, who was sick and resigned; Miller Huggins of the Yankees, who died on the job; and Connie Mack of the Athletics, who owned the club."
—SPORTSWRITER RED SMITH

• • •

"Thou shalt not steal. I mean defensively. On offense, indeed thou shall steal and thou must."
—BRANCH RICKEY, BASEBALL EXECUTIVE

• • •

"Baseball has to be a great game to survive the fools who run it."
—HALL OF FAMER BILL TERRY

• • •

"I'd rather be lucky than good."
—PITCHER RED BARRETT, BUT ALSO CREDITED TO STANDOUT PITCHER LEFTY GOMEZ

• • •

"Take nothing for granted in baseball."
—NATIONAL LEAGUE PRESIDENT HARRY PULLIAM

• • •

"Take two and hit to right."
—UNKNOWN MANAGER'S ADVICE TO A YOUNG HITTER

• • •

"Jackie Robinson is the loneliest man I have ever seen in sports."
—SPORTSWRITER ROGER KAHN, FROM HIS *THE BOYS OF SUMMER*

• • •

"You'll have to learn before you're older, you can't hit the ball with the bat on your shoulder."
—UMPIRE BILL BYRON TO A ROOKIE

• • •

"I couldn't have done it without my players."
—MANAGER CASEY STENGEL ON HIS RUN OF SUCCESS WITH THE YANKEES

• • •

"They expect an umpire to be perfect on opening day and to improve as the season goes on."
—MAJOR LEAGUE UMPIRE NESTOR CHYLAK

• • •

"Baseball is our national game."
—PRESIDENT CALVIN COOLIDGE

• • •

"Fans, for the past two weeks you have been reading about what a bad break I got. Yet today I consider myself to be the luckiest man on the face of the earth."
—YANKEES GREAT LOU GEHRIG AT YANKEE STADIUM'S "LOU GEHRIG DAY"

• • •

"I never knew how someone dying could say he was the luckiest man in the world, but now I understand."
—YANKEES GREAT MICKEY MANTLE UPON HIS RETIREMENT

• • •

"There ain't much to being a ballplayer—if you're a ballplayer."
—SHORTSTOP HONUS WAGNER

• • •

"In the beginning there was a word and the word was 'Play Ball.'"
—WRITER GEORGE BOWERING

• • •

"We'll win if the Big Dodger in the sky wills it."
—DODGER SKIPPER TOMMY LASORDA

• • •

"Hit 'em where they ain't."
—BROOKLYN'S WEE WILLIE KEELER

• • •

"Sure, I have muffed a few in my time. But I never called one wrong in my heart."
—UMPIRE BILL KLEM

• • •

"God takes care of little children and catchers."
—UNKNOWN ORIGIN

• • •

"The body of a god. Only [Mickey] Mantle's legs are mortal."
—INFIELDER JERRY COLEMAN

• • •

"I'll be home soon, Ma. The pitchers are starting to curve me."
—LINE FIRST ATTRIBUTED TO AN UNKNOWN
ROOKIE IN SPRING CAMP

• • •

"A baseball game is twice as much fun if you're seeing it on the
company's time."
—WILLIAM FEATHER, PUBLISHER

• • •

"Baseball is the only field of endeavor where a man can succeed
three times out of ten and still be considered a good performer."
—HALL OF FAMER TED WILLIAMS

• • •

"Baseball is a game of inches."
—BASEBALL EXECUTIVE BRANCH RICKEY

• • •

"Keep your eye on the ball."
—REPORTEDLY FIRST SPOKEN BY JOE SEWELL,
A PLAYER WHO STRUCK OUT 114 TIMES OVER
FOURTEEN SEASONS

• • •

"We Americans are a peculiar people. We are for the underdog no matter how much of a dog he is."
—BASEBALL COMMISSIONER HAPPY CHANDLER

• • •

"It isn't really the stars that are expensive. It's the high cost of mediocrity."
—TEAM OWNER BILL VEECK

• • •

"It's smarter to give the big man [Mickey Mantle] four balls for one base than one ball for four bases."
—FELLOW YANKEES OUTFIELDER ROGER MARIS

• • •

"The key to winning is pitching, fundamentals and three-run homers."
—ORIOLES MANAGER EARL WEAVER

• • •

"Call 'em fast and walk away tough."
—UMPIRE TIM HURST

• • •

"It's not the bat that counts. It's the guy who's wielding it."
—PAUL WANER, STAR OUTFIELDER

• • •

"It's great to be young and a Giant."
—NEW YORK GIANTS INFIELDER LARRY DOYLE

• • •

"The rhythms of the game are so similar to the patterns of American life. Periods of leisure, interrupted by bursts of frantic activity."
—WRITER ROGER KAHN

• • •

"A full mind is an empty bat."
—GENERAL MANAGER BRANCH RICKEY

• • •

"You can't teach speed."
—OLD BASEBALL ADAGE

• • •

"Rooting for the New York Yankees is like rooting for U.S. Steel."
—SPORTSWRITER RED SMITH; THIS LINE HAS ALSO BEEN ATTRIBUTED TO COMEDIAN JOE E. LEWIS

• • •

"You can't tell how much spirit a team has until it starts losing."
—TIGERS OUTFIELDER ROCKY COLAVITO

• • •

"Less than a foot can make the difference between a hero and a bum."
—PITCHING GREAT GROVER CLEVELAND ALEXANDER

• • •

"There are three things you can do in a baseball game: You can win or you can lose or it can rain."
—LEGENDARY MANAGER CASEY STENGEL

• • •

"I wish I'd known early what I had to learn late."
—PHILLIES STAR RICHIE ASHBURN

• • •

"The baseline belongs to me."
—TIGERS GREAT TY COBB

• • •

"Quick to think. Slow to anger."
—NATIONAL LEAGUE PRESIDENT WARREN GILES TO HIS UMPIRES

• • •

"I try not to break the rules but merely to test their elasticity."
—TEAM OWNER BILL VEECK

• • •

"Nice guys finish last."
—BROOKLYN MANAGER LEO DUROCHER—
ALTHOUGH ACTUALLY A MISQUOTE, THIS LINE HAS
ENDURED IN BASEBALL HISTORY.

• • •

"Age is a question of mind over matter. If you don't mind, it
doesn't matter."
—SATCHEL PAIGE

• • •

"Cut me and I'll bleed Dodger blue."
—MANAGER TOMMY LASORDA

• • •

"Wait 'til next year."
—COMMON BROOKLYN DODGERS FANS' SAYING

• • •

"We finished last with you. We can finish last without you."
—FIRST SPOKEN BY PIRATES EXECUTIVE BRANCH
RICKEY TO RALPH KINER, WHO WAS HOLDING OUT
FOR MORE MONEY

• • •

"I took two of the most expensive aspirins in history."
—FIRST BASEMAN WALLY PIPP, WHO, DUE TO A
HEADACHE, SAT OUT, WAS REPLACED BY LOU
GEHRIG, AND THEN LOST HIS JOB TO GEHRIG

• • •

"It would depend on how well she was hitting."
—PITCHER EARLY WYNN, SUPPOSEDLY
RESPONDING TO THE QUESTION, "WOULD YOU
THROW AT YOUR OWN MOTHER?"

• • •

"You gotta believe."
—RELIEVER TUG MCGRAW'S BATTLE CRY

• • •

"Because there is always some kid who may be seeing me for the
first or last time. I owe him my best."
—OUTFIELDER JOE DIMAGGIO ON WHY HE PUT
OUT 100 PERCENT EVERY GAME

• • •

"It's nothin' till I call it."
—ASSERTIVE UMPIRE BILL KLEM

• • •

"I have discovered, in twenty years of moving around a ballpark,
that the knowledge of the game is usually in inverse proportion
to the price of the seats."
—TEAM OWNER BILL VEECK

• • •

"Close don't count in baseball. Close only counts in horseshoes
and grenades."
—OUTFIELDER FRANK ROBINSON

• • •

"This must be the only job in America that everybody knows
how to do better than the guy who's doing it."
—UMPIRE NESTOR CHYLAK

• • •

"Ninety feet between home plate and first base may be the closest
man has ever come to perfection."
—SPORTSWRITER RED SMITH

• • •

"There's nothing wrong with this club that a few wins won't cure."
—UNKNOWN

• • •

"Let him hit you—you've got fielders behind you."
—BASEBALL PIONEER ALEXANDER CARTWRIGHT

• • •

"Champions cost money."
—A'S OWNER CONNIE MACK

• • •

PART TWO

Humor

Clearly baseball is the perfect game for humor. Long rain delays provide time and a built-in audience for the clowns and wits of baseball. There is more leisurely down time in baseball than most sports—time for players, managers, coaches, and the media to shoot the breeze. Not only that, but often when men have so much time to chat, you can bet there will be a lot of serious talk about baseball, a lot about women, and a lot of funny stuff left over.

The humor of baseball is as old as the game itself. In this chapter you will find a quote from as far back as the 1890s from right fielder King Kelly and other quips and comments two centuries removed from Kelly. Colorful nicknames in baseball may have gone the way of nickel candy bars, but the humor endures.

Some of the clown princes of the game have generated tons of hilarious quotes. A Hall of Fame in this department would have to include Bob Uecker, Yogi Berra, Casey Stengel, Andy Van Slyke, Dizzy Dean, Rocky Bridges, Joe Garagiola, and Lefty Gomez. However, you'll also come across a gem or two from somewhat lesser-known wits such as Toby Harrah, with his classic line on statistics being like a girl in a bikini. For that matter, pitcher Tommy John, much more widely known for his mound skill than his humor, came up with a great, subtle line to a reporter concerning a home run he once dished up.

Like a Whitman sampler, this chapter is chock-full of goodies from the men mentioned above and lots more. It should prove to be delectable reading.

One final note—in some cases there is a thin distinction between the brand of humor displayed in this chapter and the ones coming later in the chapter on "wacky" humor. Ultimately, this should be a case of "Who cares?" in that the main purpose of the line is to entertain, so there's no need to fret about labels here. Simply sit back and enjoy the rich humor of the game.

● ● ●

"In 1967 with St. Louis, I walked with the bases loaded to drive in the winning run in an intrasquad game in spring training."
—CATCHER BOB UECKER JOKING ABOUT HIS BIGGEST BASEBALL THRILL

• • •

"The biggest adjustment from the minor leagues to the major leagues is learning how to spend the $45 in meal money a day."
—PIRATES OUTFIELDER ANDY VAN SLYKE

• • •

"When the Supreme Court says baseball isn't run like a business, everybody jumps up and down with joy. When I say the same thing, everybody throws pointy objects at me."
—TEAM OWNER BILL VEECK, FROM HIS BOOK *THE HUSTLER'S HANDBOOK* (WRITTEN WITH ED LINN)

• • •

"Why, they shot the wrong McKinley."
—PITCHER DIZZY DEAN TO UMPIRE WILLIAM MCKINLEY

• • •

"I enjoyed hitting. I just didn't make contact too often."
—PITCHER BOB BUHL, A LIFETIME .089 HITTER

• • •

"I tell George [Steinbrenner] what I think and then I do what he says."
—YANKEES MANAGER BOB LEMON ON HIS BOSS

• • •

"All the fat guys watch me and say to their wives, 'See, there's a fat guy doing okay. Bring me another beer.'"
—PORTLY PITCHER MICKEY LOLICH

• • •

"I don't wanna throw nothin'. Maybe he'll get tired of waiting and leave."
—COLORFUL PITCHER LEFTY GOMEZ WHEN ASKED BY HIS CATCHER WHY HE CONTINUED TO SHAKE OFF SIGN AFTER SIGN AFTER SIGN WHILE FACING JIMMIE FOXX

• • •

"I always liked working Indians games, because they were usually out of the pennant race by the end of April and there was never too much pressure on the umpires."
—RON LUCIANO, UMPIRE, FROM HIS *THE UMPIRE STRIKES BACK*

• • •

"We've got to learn to stay out of triple plays."
—METS MANAGER CASEY STENGEL, LOOKING AHEAD TO THE 1963 SEASON AFTER ENDING THEIR INITIAL SEASON ON A TRIPLE PLAY

• • •

"If we hadn't won I would have jumped off a tall building. But the way I'm hitting, I wouldn't have hit the ground anyway."
—INFIELDER PHIL GARNER AFTER HITTING INTO A TRIPLE PLAY

• • •

"After the game, there'll be more food for everyone."
—ORIOLES PITCHER TIPPY MARTINEZ ON THE RAMIFICATIONS OF THE TRADE OF TIM STODDARD, 6' 7", 250-PLUS POUNDS

• • •

"A waist is a terrible thing to mind."
—BURLY PITCHER TERRY FORSTER

• • •

"Children have been conceived and born during a Mike Hargrove at bat."
—ANNOUNCER NORM HITZGES

• • •

"It's a good thing I stayed in Cincinnati for four years—it took me that long to learn how to spell it."
—INFIELDER ROCKY BRIDGES

• • •

"The Mets achieved total incompetence in a single year, while the Browns worked industriously for almost a decade to gain equal proficiency."
—ST. LOUIS BROWNS OWNER BILL VEECK, FROM *VEECK AS IN WRECK* BY VEECK AND ED LINN

• • •

"Our similarities are different."
—INFIELDER DALE BERRA ON HIS FATHER YOGI

• • •

"It was after he hit it."
—PITCHER TOMMY JOHN WHEN ASKED IF A PITCH HE SERVED UP FOR A HOMER WAS OUT OF THE STRIKE ZONE

• • •

"Every time I sign a ball, and there must have been thousands, I thank my luck that I wasn't born Coveleski or Wambsganss or Peckinpaugh."
—SLUGGER MEL OTT

• • •

"I go back to 1965 with Reggie [Jackson], but I guess I don't go back far enough to remember when he was shy."
—OUTFIELDER RICK MONDAY

• • •

"Statistics are like a girl in a bikini. They show a lot, but not everything."
—INFIELDER TOBY HARRAH

• • •

"If we're going to run away from Toronto, first we've got to catch them and go by them."
—YANKEES CATCHER MIKE STANLEY

• • •

"We have a lot of pitchers capable of stopping our win streak."
—RED SOX HURLER BRUCE HURST

• • •

"Most Valuable Player on the worst team ever? Just how did they mean that?"
—A PERPLEXED RICHIE ASHBURN, NAMED THE 1962 METS TEAM MVP

• • •

"Looks like Tarzan. Runs like Jane."
—SCOUTING REPORT ON AN UNIDENTIFIED PLAYER

• • •

"300 Wins is Nothing to Spit At."
—SAYING PITCHER GAYLORD PERRY WORE ON HIS T-SHIRT THE DAY HE NOTCHED HIS HISTORIC WIN

• • •

"It's easy to beat the shift. All you got to do is hit it in the stands."
—INDIANS HITTING COACH CLARENCE JONES

• • •

"I'll tell you how smart Pete Rose is. When they had the blackout in New York, he was stranded thirteen hours on an escalator."
—FORMER PITCHER JOE NUXHALL

• • •

"Sure I do, and if someone paid you $6,000 a game, you'd have fun, too."
—PHILLIES STAR PETE ROSE WHEN ASKED IF HE HAS FUN PLAYING BASEBALL

• • •

"Bobo Newsom claims we had a gentlemen's agreement on his contract. Couldn't be. No gentlemen were involved."
—MINOR LEAGUE TEAM OWNER JOE ENGEL

• • •

"He's spent several years in the majors plus several more with the Pirates."
—YANKEES STAR DON MATTINGLY ON PITCHER RICK RHODEN

• • •

"It was said that the first book Mickey Mantle ever finished was his own autobiography."
—AUTHOR JOSEPH MCBRIDE

• • •

"The Goose [Rich Gossage] should do more pitching and less quacking."
—YANKEES OWNER GEORGE STEINBRENNER

• • •

"I've buried people in better shape than I'm in."
—THIRD BASEMAN RICHIE HEBNER, AN OFFSEASON GRAVE DIGGER

• • •

"You can't get rich sitting on the bench, but I'm giving it a try."
—UTILITY PLAYER PHIL LINZ

• • •

"Hating the New York Yankees is as American as apple pie, unwed mothers, and cheating on your income tax."
—JOURNALIST MIKE ROYKO

• • •

"You never know with these psychosomatic injuries. You have to take your time with them."
—ORIOLES PITCHER JIM PALMER

• • •

"I'm getting smarter, I finally punched something that couldn't sue me."
—A'S MANAGER BILLY MARTIN, AFTER PUNCHING A PIECE OF FURNITURE

• • •

"That's pretty good, considering Dave's previous idol was himself."
—PIRATES STAR WILLIE STARGELL, WHEN TOLD TEAMMATE DAVE PARKER LISTED STARGELL AS HIS IDOL

• • •

"Boys, I'm one of those umpires that can make a mistake on the close ones. So, if it's close, you'd better hit it."
—UMPIRE CAL HUBBARD

• • •

"I always felt the more [St. Louis] Browns I could place on the other teams, the better off we would be."
—TEAM OWNER BILL VEECK ON WHY HE TRADED SO MANY OF HIS BROWNS

• • •

"Chuck Tanner used to have a bed check just for me every night. No problem—my bed was always there."
—PIRATES PITCHER JIM ROOKER

• • •

"I'm going to write a book: *How to Make a Small Fortune in Baseball*. You start with a large fortune."
—TEAM OWNER RULY CARPENTER

• • •

"What do you want, a bonus or a limp?"
—DODGERS EXECUTIVE FRESCO THOMPSON ON
WHY A PLAYER HIS TEAM HAD SCOUTED SHOULD
SIGN TO PLAY BASEBALL INSTEAD OF FOOTBALL

• • •

"If you approach Billy Martin right, he's okay. I avoid him altogether."
—YANKEE PITCHER RON GUIDRY ON HIS SKIPPER

• • •

"If everybody on this team commenced breaking up the furniture every time we did bad, there'd be no place to sit."
—CASEY STENGEL, MANAGER OF THE PATHETIC METS

• • •

"I can see the sun okay and that's 93,000,000 miles away."
—UMPIRE BRUCE FROEMMING ON HOW GOOD HIS EYESIGHT IS

• • •

"Yes, and so is everyone else in the league."
—COMEDIAN GROUCHO MARX WHEN TOLD THAT
LEO DUROCHER WAS LEADING THE GIANTS

• • •

"Felt pretty good when I got up this morning, but I got over it."
—CATCHER SMOKY BURGESS

• • •

"He couldn't hit a curve ball with an ironing board."
—PITCHER BOB FELLER ON NBA STAR MICHAEL
JORDAN'S ATTEMPT TO MAKE IT IN BASEBALL

• • •

"Oh, until about five minutes after I'm dead."
—BILL SHEA, LAWYER (WHO HELPED NEW YORK
GET A NATIONAL LEAGUE CLUB, THE METS, AFTER
THE CITY HAD LOST THE DODGERS AND GIANTS)
WHEN ASKED HOW LONG HE THOUGHT THE TEAM
WOULD CONTINUE TO NAME THEIR STADIUM
AFTER HIM

• • •

"When Manny [Sanguillen] takes a pitch, it's either a wild pitch
or paralysis has set in."
—PIRATES GENERAL MANAGER JOE BROWN ON HIS
FREE-SWINGING CATCHER

• • •

"Chicago Cubs fans are the greatest fans in baseball—they have to be."
—CUBS MANAGER HERMAN FRANKS

• • •

"Baseball is like this. Have one good year and you can fool them for five more, because for five more years they expect you to have another good one."
—MANAGER FRANKIE FRISCH

• • •

"They should move first base back a step to eliminate all the close plays."
—OUTFIELDER/DESIGNATED HITTER JOHN LOWENSTEIN

• • •

"I'll play first, third, left. I'll play anywhere—except Philadelphia."
—SLUGGER DICK ALLEN

• • •

"It's a hard slider."
—PITCHER GAYLORD PERRY'S DAUGHTER, FIVE-YEAR-OLD ALLISON, WHEN ASKED IF HER DADDY THREW A SPITBALL

• • •

"I believe if 'Shoeless' Joe Jackson were playing today, he'd have a shoe contract."
—YANKEES STAR DON MATTINGLY

• • •

"I have a son and I make him watch the Mets. I want him to know life. It's a history lesson. He'll understand the Depression when they teach it to him in school."
—FAMOUS RESTAURANT OWNER TOOTS SHOR ON THE EARLY, PATHETIC METS

• • •

"He looks like a guy who went to fantasy camp and decided to stay."
—FORMER PITCHER DON SUTTON ON PUDGY OUTFIELDER JOHN KRUK

• • •

"Bob Gibson is the luckiest pitcher I ever saw. He always pitches when the other team doesn't score any runs."
—GIBSON'S CATCHER, TIM MCCARVER

• • •

"As a nation we are dedicated to keeping physically fit—and parking as close to the stadium as possible."
—WRITER BILL VAUGHAN

• • •

"I didn't want Dr. Jobe building a swimming pool
with my knee."
—PITCHER STEVE HOWE ON WHY HE REFUSED TO
UNDERGO SURGERY

• • •

"The reason the Yankees never lay an egg is because they don't
operate on chicken feed."
—WRITER DAN PARKER

• • •

"This team finished last on merit."
—FRONT OFFICE MAN BRANCH RICKEY ON HIS
HAPLESS PIRATES OF 1952

• • •

"Tug McGraw has about forty-eight cards in his deck."
—PITCHER TOM SEAVER, A MCGRAW TEAMMATE
ON THE METS

• • •

"I'm the most loyal player money can buy."
—PITCHER DON SUTTON

• • •

"It couldn't have happened to a greater guy. Well, yes, it could. It
could have happened to me."
—DODGERS MANAGER TOMMY LASORDA AFTER HIS
PITCHER, JERRY REUSS, THREW A NO-HITTER

• • •

"Son, we'd like to keep you around this season, but we're going to try to win a pennant."
—YANKEES MANAGER CASEY STENGEL TO ROOKIE AUBREY GATEWOOD

• • •

"I've always done what was best for the club. Like this week, when I retired."
—RELIEVER KENT TEKULVE

• • •

"The only thing worse than a Mets game is a Mets doubleheader."
—CASEY STENGEL, MANAGER OF THE WOEFUL METS

• • •

"Baseball is like church. Many attend, but few understand."
—WES WESTRUM, BIG LEAGUE MANAGER

• • •

"I was very calm. What are they going to do if I don't get a hit? Bench me?"
—PINCH HITTER BILL NAHORODNY

• • •

"Being traded is like celebrating your hundredth birthday. It might not be the happiest occasion in the world, but consider the alternatives."
—SPORTSCASTER JOE GARAGIOLA

• • •

"When I'm on the road, my greatest ambition is to get a standing boo."
—RELIEVER AL HRABOSKY

• • •

"I was not successful as a ball player, as it was a game of skill."
—SUCCESSFUL MANAGER CASEY STENGEL

• • •

"Tell you what, you keep the salary and pay me the cut."
—LEFTY GOMEZ, PITCHER, WHEN TOLD TO SIGN A CONTRACT CUTTING HIS SALARY BY $12,500, DOWN FROM $20,000

• • •

"The doctor asked me the day of the week and I said, 'Friday.' Then he asked me who was the President of the United States. I said, 'Hell, I didn't know that *before* I hit my head.'"
—DON ZIMMER, INFIELDER, AFTER HE HAD FALLEN ON HIS HEAD

• • •

"How do you know when George Steinbrenner is lying? When you see his lips move."
—WHITE SOX EXECUTIVE JERRY REINSDORF

• • •

"A heck of a lot better than being the smallest player in the minors."
—FRED PATEK, 5'4" SHORTSTOP, WHEN ASKED HOW IT FELT TO BE THE SMALLEST PLAYER IN THE MAJORS

• • •

"When the year was over they wanted to give me back as the player to be named later."
—OUTFIELDER RICHIE SCHEINBLUM

• • •

"The toughest call an umpire has to make is not the half-swing; the toughest call is throwing a guy out of the game after you blew the hell out of the play."
—UMPIRE JOHNNY RICE

• • •

"The fans like to see home runs and we have assembled a pitching staff for their enjoyment."
—TWINS EXECUTIVE CLARK GRIFFITH

• • •

"I wanted to go into my home run trot, but I realized I didn't have one."
—WHITE SOX CATCHER JIM ESSIAN ON HIS FIRST BIG LEAGUE HOME RUN

• • •

"Umpiring is best described as the profession of standing between two seven-year-olds with one ice cream cone."
—FORMER UMPIRE RON LUCIANO

• • •

"You have to give him credit. Most guys don't start cheating until later in their career."
—CUBS' MARK GRACE ON A YOUNG PITCHER CAUGHT LOADING UP ON A PITCH

• • •

"It depends on the length of the game."
—HALL OF FAMER KING KELLY WHEN ASKED IF HE DRINKS WHILE PLAYING

• • •

"In Cleveland, pennant fever usually ends up being just a forty-eight-hour virus."
—FRANK ROBINSON, HALL OF FAME OUTFIELDER

• • •

"If you can't stand the heat, stay out of The Chicken."
—TED GIANNOULAS, THE MAN WHO FOR YEARS WAS THE PADRES MASCOT, THE SAN DIEGO CHICKEN, ON A SCORCHING HOT DAY

• • •

"When they operated, I told them to put in a Koufax fastball.
They did, but it was a Mrs. Koufax fastball."
—PITCHER TOMMY JOHN ON HIS ARM OPERATION

• • •

"He should have been better, pitching on 3,195 days' rest."
—SPORTSCASTER STEVE BLASS ON A PITCHER WHO
HAD BEEN OUT OF THE GAME FOR ALMOST NINE
SEASONS

• • •

"I'm superstitious and every night after I got a hit, I ate Chinese
food and drank tequila. I had to stop hitting or die."
—METS INFIELDER ED CHARLES

• • •

"If everyone contributes what their agents say they'll contribute,
we'll have 172 wins and no losses."
—CLEVELAND MANAGER DAVE GARCIA

• • •

"When you're twenty-one, you're a prospect. When you're thirty,
you're a suspect."
—PITCHER JIM MCGLOTHLIN

• • •

"He certainly has turned his life around. He used to be depressed and miserable. Now he's miserable and depressed."
—PHILLIES ANNOUNCER HARRY KALAS ON PHILADELPHIA'S CENTER FIELDER GARY MADDOX

• • •

"The whole thing reminded me of the junior prom—not a lot of action; just a lot of guys standing around, watching what's going on."
—PITCHER DAN QUISENBERRY ON A "BRAWL"

• • •

"The average age of our bench is deceased."
—DODGERS MANAGER TOMMY LASORDA

• • •

"I refuse to call a fifty-two-year-old man Sparky."
—UMPIRE AL CLARK ON HIS INSISTENCE ON CALLING SPARKY ANDERSON BY HIS REAL FIRST NAME, GEORGE

• • •

"We know we're better than this, but we can't prove it."
—PADRES STAR TONY GWYNN DURING A LONG LOSING STREAK

• • •

"If he raced his pregnant wife, he'd finish third."
—TOMMY LASORDA, DODGERS MANAGER, ON HIS
CATCHER, MIKE SCIOSCIA

• • •

"The kid doesn't chew tobacco, smoke, drink, curse, or chase
broads. I don't see how he can possibly make it."
—HALL OF FAMER RICHIE ASHBURN ON A PHILLIES
ROOKIE

• • •

"I occasionally get birthday cards from fans. But it's often the
same message—they hope it's my last."
—UMPIRE AL FORMAN

• • •

"We forgot about the Canadian exchange rate, so its really only
82 mph."
—INFIELDER TIM FLANNERY UPON LEARNING
THAT TEAMMATE MIKE BODDICKER WAS
REPORTEDLY THROWING THE BALL AT 88 MPH
DURING A GAME IN TORONTO

• • •

"It was a baseball."
—WHITE SOX HURLER JOE HORLEN, WHEN ASKED
WHAT HE HAD THROWN TO TONY CONIGLIARO
WHO HAD HOMERED TO WIN A 1-0 GAME

• • •

"We live by the Golden Rule—those who have the gold make the rules."
—BASEBALL EXECUTIVE BUZZIE BAVASI

• • •

"I'll never make the mistake of being seventy years old again."
—LEGENDARY MANAGER CASEY STENGEL AFTER BEING FIRED DUE TO HIS AGE

• • •

"He can hit just as good right-handed as he can left-handed. He's just naturally amphibious."
—YOGI BERRA ON SWITCH HITTER MICKEY MANTLE

• • •

"A couple of years ago they told me I was too young to be President and you were too old to be playing baseball, but we fooled them."
—UNITED STATES PRESIDENT JOHN F. KENNEDY TO ST. LOUIS GREAT STAN MUSIAL

• • •

"Anytime I got those bang-bang plays at first base, I called them out. It made the game shorter."
—UMPIRE TOM GORMAN

• • •

"One of them has me dead already."
—INFIELDER MARK KOENIG ON WHY HE DOESN'T TRUST BOOKS WRITTEN ABOUT HIS 1927 YANKEES

• • •

PART THREE

The Media

Ted Williams had disdain for the men of the press box, calling them the "Knights of the Keyboard," and certainly some reporters deserved such disrespect. Some would even slit a proverbial throat or two to get a scoop. Misquoting a source is yet another sin committed by some members of the media, as is the occasional breeching of players' trust. Just ask taciturn Steve Carlton, who clammed up for an eon, refusing to open up for the media until he was voted into the Hall of Fame.

Those indiscretions aside, credit is due to so many members of the media who have enriched the game of baseball with their wit, assiduity, and, of course, their prose. These men elevate an already beautiful and vibrant game to a grand, even poetic level. We listen to and read the words of these men with rapt attention and interest.

Over the years the relationship of fans and their hometown team's announcers has been intimate. Fans fall in love with their "guy," be he a "homer," one who unabashedly roots on air for his team (e.g. Bob Prince and his Pirates over the air waves of station KDKA, the very station that carried the first broadcast of a big league game) or one who is more objective, more of an observer and a reporter of facts (along the lines of a Vin Scully, who has spun words and tales for decades now), and there's also room for a man such as Harry Caray, who could get away with ripping a Chicago player for disappointing suffering Cubs fans with a bone-headed play, for example.

We have even elevated the scribes and voices of the game to Hall of Fame status.

Furthermore, even those of us who grew up thousands of miles out of the radio range of a Mel Allen, Red Barber, Jack Buck, or Ernie Harwell know of these legends. Similarly, readers today can appreciate the craft of writers long gone, the giants of journalism such as Red Smith, Ring Lardner, and Jim Murray.

So, while some throwaway, impermanent words of the media are meant to be read or listened to then quickly forgotten, discarded like the words a child might scrawl on an Etch-A-Sketch and then eradicate with a few flicks of the hands, the words of the men that follow deserve to be indelible ones, worthy of Rosetta Stone status.

• • •

"I have a theory—the larger the ball, the less writing about the sport. There are superb books about golf, very good books about baseball, not many books about football, and very few books about basketball. There are no books about beachballs."
—AUTHOR GEORGE PLIMPTON

• • •

"Today's players are more concerned about what the press says; those guys [from the Babe Ruth era] didn't care. Those guys long ago didn't really care that much about it [because] a lot of them couldn't read."
—ORIOLES COACH ELROD HENDRICKS

• • •

"Casey's memory is legendary. It's also inaccurate."
—AUTHOR ED LINN ON CASEY STENGEL

• • •

"They discovered 'boo' is pronounced the same in French as it is in English."
—CUBS ANNOUNCER HARRY CARAY ON BASEBALL'S FRANCHISE IN MONTREAL

• • •

"If Casey Stengel were alive today, he'd be spinning in his grave."
—METS ANNOUNCER RALPH KINER

• • •

"Baseball is a game where a curve is an optical illusion, a screw-ball can be a pitch or a person, stealing is legal, and you can spit anywhere you like except in the umpire's eye or on the ball."
—SPORTSWRITER JIM MURRAY

• • •

"[Duke] Snider, [Mickey] Mantle, and [Willie] Mays—you could get a fat lip in any saloon by starting an argument as to which was best. One point was beyond argument, though. Willie was by all odds the most exciting."
—RED SMITH, SPORTSWRITER

• • •

"It is interesting about people that leave early from ballgames: It's almost as if they came out to the ballgame to see if they can beat the traffic home."
—OAKLAND A'S ANNOUNCER LON SIMMONS

• • •

"He [Mark McGwire] doesn't want to talk about the past [at Congressional hearings on steroid use]? I don't want to consider his past."
—DAYTON DAILY NEWS WRITER HAL MCCOY IN 2006 ON WHY HE WOULDN'T VOTE FOR MCGWIRE FOR HALL OF FAME CONSIDERATION

• • •

"It doesn't make any difference. They [female reporters] don't ask any dumber questions than the guys do."
—ANGELS MANAGER JIM FREGOSI WHEN FEMALE WRITERS WERE FIRST PERMITTED IN THE LOCKER ROOM IN 1979

• • •

"Baseball is a peculiar profession, possibly the only one which capitalizes on a boyhood pleasure, unfits the athlete for any other career, keeps him young in mind and spirit, and then rejects him as too old before he has yet attained the prime of his life."
—JOURNALIST GERALD BEAUMONT

• • •

"Statistics are used like a drunk uses a lamp post—for support, not illumination."
—DODGERS ANNOUNCER VIN SCULLY

• • •

"Hell, if the game was half as complicated as some of these writers make out it is, a lot of us boys from the farm would never have been able to make a living at it."
—PITCHER BUCKY WALTERS

• • •

"The Red Sox truly are the boys of summer; it's always been the fall that's given them trouble."
—BOSTON WRITER DAN SHAUGHNESSY

• • •

"There are days when you know that God invented baseball to give us all a concept of eternity, when the game moves so slowly that it hangs heavy as a beer-bloated belly."
—WRITER MICHAEL OLESKER OF THE *BALTIMORE SUN*

• • •

"I really love baseball. The guys and the game and I love the challenge of describing things. The only thing I hate . . . is the loneliness of the road."
—DODGERS ANNOUNCER VIN SCULLY

• • •

"When you hold the ball between your thumb and forefinger you can hear a rabbit's pulsebeat."
—COLUMNIST WESTBROOK PEGLER ON THE LIVELY BALL OF THE 1920S

• • •

"It's not whether you win or lose, it's how you play the game."
—SPORTSWRITER GRANTLAND RICE

• • •

"You can kiss it goodbye."
—PIRATES ANNOUNCER BOB PRINCE'S HOME RUN CALL

• • •

"A man opposed to Sunday baseball except when the gate receipts exceeded $5,000."
—SPORTSWRITER RING LARDNER, DESCRIBING TEAM EXECUTIVE BRANCH RICKEY

• • •

"When I was in baseball and you went into the clubhouse, you didn't see ballplayers with curling irons."
—RETIRED ANNOUNCER RED BARBER

• • •

"Gene Mauch was one of the great managers I played for. He'd say, 'Uecker, grab a bat and stop this rally.'"
—ANNOUNCER AND FORMER CATCHER BOB UECKER

• • •

"The rain is coming down hard now. Although, I guess the real story would be if the rain was going up."
—ANNOUNCER TOMMY HUTTON

• • •

"[Connie Mack] has been baseball's high priest and patriarch, one of its keenest minds, its priceless ambassador, one of its sharpest businessmen, certainly its most indestructible myth."
—SPORTSWRITER RED SMITH, FROM *THE RED SMITH READER,* EDITED BY DAVE ANDERSON

• • •

"All literary men are Red Sox fans. To be a Yankee fan in literary society is to endanger your life."
—NOVELIST JOHN CHEEVER

• • •

"How good was Stan Musial? He was good enough to take your breath away."
—DODGERS BROADCASTER VIN SCULLY

• • •

"What the hell do they need quotes for? They all saw the play."
—OUTFIELDER TOMMY HARPER

• • •

"That's easy. You just take a gun and shoot him."
—WRITER RING LARDNER ON HOW TO STOP TY COBB

• • •

"A baseball game is simply a nervous breakdown divided into nine innings."
—WRITER EARL WILSON

• • •

"Writing a column is easy. All you do every day is sit down to a typewriter, open a vein and bleed."
—SPORTSWRITER RED SMITH

• • •

"How 'bout that, sports fans?"
—LEGENDARY ANNOUNCER MEL ALLEN

• • •

"Since 1946, the Cubs have had two problems: They put too few runs on the scoreboard and the other guys put too many. So what is the new management improving? The scoreboard."
—WRITER GEORGE F. WILL

• • •

"Ballplayers shouldn't gripe about reporters. A ballplayer should stay on a reporter's good side. Say nice things. Admire his clothes. Compliment him on his T-shirt."
—OUTFIELDER ANDY VAN SLYKE

• • •

"Baseball is a story that weaves itself through every single day of its season."
—BROADCASTER AL MICHAELS

• • •

"Baseball is the best sport for a writer to cover, because it's daily. It's ongoing. You have to fill the need, write the daily soap opera."
—PETER GAMMONS OF THE *BOSTON GLOBE*

• • •

"Now it is done. Now the story ends. And there is no way to tell it. The art of fiction is dead. Reality has strangled invention. Only the utterly impossible, the inexpressibly fantastic, can ever be possible again."
—SPORTSWRITER RED SMITH ON BOBBY THOMSON'S HOMER TO CLINCH THE PENNANT FOR THE DODGERS IN 1951

• • •

"They're tearing up the pea patch."
—ANNOUNCER RED BARBER, WHEN HIS DODGERS WERE SCORING RUNS

• • •

"Baseball players who are first into the dining room are usually last in statistics."
—SPORTSWRITER JIMMY CANNON

• • •

"It's going, going, gone."
—FIRST ATTRIBUTED TO ANNOUNCER MEL ALLEN (AS HIS CLASSIC HOME RUN CALL)

• • •

"A ballplayer has two reputations, one with the other players and one with the fans. The first is based on ability. The second the newspapers give him."
—CUBS INFIELDER JOHNNY EVERS

• • •

"Cubs win! Cubs win! Cubs win!"
—ANNOUNCER HARRY CARAY

• • •

"I know a thousand times more about this game than you and what I know, I can't explain to you guys."
—ROYALS MANAGER BOB BOONE TO THE MEDIA

• • •

"Any person claiming to be a baseball fan who does not also claim to have invented the quickest, simplest, and most complete method of keeping score probably is a fraud."
—WRITER THOMAS BOSWELL

• • •

"Oh, Doctor!"
—PET PHRASE OF ANNOUNCER RED BARBER

• • •

"I try to have respect for people in general, whether it's baseball players or low lifes like the media."
—JIM RIGGLEMAN, AS MANAGER OF THE CUBS

• • •

"He is easily the slowest ballplayer since Ernie Lombardi was thrown out at first base trying to stretch a double into a single."
—SPORTSWRITER STANLEY FRANK ON LOU BOUDREAU

• • •

"Until I saw [Mickey] Mantle peel down for his shower in the clubhouse at Comiskey Park one afternoon, I never knew how he developed his brutal power, but his bare back looked like a barrelful of snakes."
—SPORTS COLUMNIST DALE LANCASTER

• • •

"There is something uniquely American in hitting one out of the park."
—NEWSPAPER WRITER DICK YOUNG

• • •

"Cubs fans are 90 percent scar tissue."
—WRITER GEORGE F. WILL

• • •

"Cheating is baseball's oldest profession. No other game is so rich in skulduggery, so suited for it or so proud of it."
—WRITER THOMAS BOSWELL, FROM *INSIDE SPORTS*

• • •

"Baseball isn't a life-and-death matter, but the Red Sox are."
—BOSTON WRITER MIKE BARNICLE

• • •

"We had 'em all the way."
—PIRATES ANNOUNCER BOB PRINCE, OFTEN SAID JOKINGLY AFTER EKING OUT A CLOSE WIN

• • •

"A mouse studying to be a rat."
—CHICAGO WRITER JOHN SCHULIAN ON BILLY
MARTIN

• • •

"Baseball is dull only to those with dull minds."
—SPORTSWRITER RED SMITH

• • •

"He's got a gun concealed about his person. They can't tell me he
throws them balls with his arm."
—WRITER RING LARDNER OF WALTER JOHNSON'S
FASTBALL

• • •

"Holy cow!"
—CLASSIC CALL OF YANKEES ANNOUNCER PHIL
RIZZUTO

• • •

"The only difference between the Mets and the Titanic is that the
Mets have a better organist."
—WRITER JIM MURRAY

• • •

"He slud into third."
—DIZZY DEAN AS A BROADCASTER

• • •

"You've got to be careful. Most writers are good guys, but there's always one in a crowd, one who tries to quote you out of context, to make you look bad, and you've got to look around for him."
—TIGERS SUPERSTAR AL KALINE

• • •

"Catching a fly ball, or hitting a curved one, is not all that difficult. It may rank in difficulty somewhere below juggling Indian clubs and above playing an ocarina."
—SPORTSWRITER JIM MURRAY

• • •

"How could it have been a perfect game? It was in Cleveland."
—SPORTSWRITER RANDY GALLOWAY ON LEN BARKER'S GEM IN 1981

• • •

"It may be that the race is not always to the swift nor the battle to the strong—but that is the way to bet."
—SPORTSWRITER DAMON RUNYON

• • •

"The new breed of writers are looking for social significance. They dwell too much on whether a player is getting along with a manager or how happy he is at home. They ought to be writing for the gossip columns, not the baseball fans."
—BRAVES EXECUTIVE PAUL RICHARDS, 1969

• • •

"I haven't missed a game in two and a half years. I go to the park sick as a dog and, when I see my uniform hanging there, I get well right now. Then I see some of you [media] guys and I get sick again."
—CINCINNATI'S PETE ROSE

• • •

"For the next twenty years, I believed that the three worst people of the twentieth century were Hitler, Stalin and Walter O'Malley. I never forgave any of them."
—PETE HAMILL, NEW YORK WRITER, ON O'MALLEY, WHO MOVED THE DODGERS OUT OF BROOKLYN

• • •

"Nothing on earth is more depressing than an old baseball writer."
—RING LARDNER, SPORTSWRITER

• • •

"Sometimes they write what I say and not what I mean."
—DODGERS OUTFIELDER PEDRO GUERRERO

• • •

"Sports is the toy department of life."
—SPORTSWRITER JIMMY CANNON

• • •

"Has anybody ever satisfactorily explained why the bad hop is always the last one?"
—GIANTS SPORTSCASTER HANK GREENWALD

• • •

"It's a mere moment in a man's life between the All-Star game and an old-timer's game."
—DODGER BROADCASTER VIN SCULLY

• • •

"Baseball owners have moral scruples against taking any man's dollar when there is a chance to take a dollar and a quarter."
—SPORTSWRITER RED SMITH

• • •

"If asked where baseball stood amid such notions as country, family, love, honor, art, and religion, we might say derisively, 'Just a game.' But, under oath, I'd abandon some of those Big Six before I'd give up baseball."
—WRITER THOMAS BOSWELL

• • •

"We need a bloop and a blast."
—PIRATES ANNOUNCER BOB PRINCE

• • •

"The only way you can get along with newspapermen is to say something one minute and something different the next."
—TIGERS STAR HANK GREENBERG

• • •

"He is what Norman Rockwell would draw for a *Saturday Evening Post* cover if he was doing a ballplayer. Pete [Rose] looks as if he should have a dog with him."
—SPORTSWRITER JIM MURRAY

• • •

"Let's check the scoreboard, brought to you by Subway sandwiches. It's still there."
—GIANTS BROADCASTER HANK GREENWALD AT A TIME WHEN NO OTHER CONTESTS WERE GOING ON

• • •

"The last time Willie Mays dropped a pop fly he had a rattle in one hand and a bonnet on his head."
—SPORTSWRITER JIM MURRAY

• • •

"This isn't just a ball club. This is Murderers' Row."
—NEW YORK WRITER ARTHUR ROBINSON ON THE YANKEES

• • •

"If it isn't, General Motors is a sport."
—SPORTSWRITER JIM MURRAY ON WHETHER BASEBALL IS A BUSINESS OR NOT

• • •

"The Lord taught me to love everybody. But the last ones I learned to love were the sportswriters."
—OAKLAND MANAGER ALVIN DARK

• • •

"Anyone who thinks he can run baseball without a daily paper, can't run baseball."
—BROOKLYN DODGERS OWNER WALTER O'MALLEY

• • •

"The Dodgers are such a .500 club, they could probably split a three-game series."
—ANNOUNCER VIN SCULLY

• • •

"He [Red Barber] reminds me of the Arabian horse. Every thoroughbred racehorse in the world is descended from the Arabian. Every announcer learned something from Red."
—DODGERS EXECUTIVE BUZZIE BAVASI

• • •

"I don't get mad at the writers. I used to, but I found out that most of the things they say, critical or not, are true."
—OUTFIELDER MIKE VAIL

• • •

PART FOUR

Hitters and Hitting

Legendary hitting instructor Charlie Lau once said, "Nobody should hit .200. Anybody should [be able to] hit .250." In theory, perhaps, but in this chapter quotes flow not only from the stars of the game who soared well above the .200 and .250 strata, but also from a few men who would have infuriated Lau (initially and/or for their entire careers). There are even some observations from pitchers.

Hitting, after all, is a skill that has been studied for many a decade now, with some calling the study a science and others insisting hitting is more of an art. In any event, the topic has fascinated both players and fans alike since the dawn of the game.

For a man like Joe DiMaggio, hitting involved, as he put it, no skill at all: "Just go up there and swing at the ball." Easy for him to say; this was a lifetime .325 hitter. For others like pitcher Bob Buhl, hitting the ball crisply is a nearly impossible task.

Further, while pitching may well be the name of the game, fans, by and large, pack the ballparks to see hitters. Sure, many *claim* they love nothing better than taking in a classic pitchers' duel, but box office receipts belie that assertion and when baseball needs to boost attendance, they've been known to juice the ball or devise rules to shift the advantage to hitters.

There's a direct correlation between eras of hitting dominance and the rapid-fire clicking of big league turnstiles. Look no further than the record-setting attendance figures of the late 1990s and into the 21st century.

Of course, we could look way back in time, too. The demise of the dead-ball era, with none other than Babe Ruth dramatically plunging a knife into that period of baseball history with his long-ball exploits (an unheard of 29 homers in 1919, then an incredible 54 in 1920, followed by an ungodly 60 in 1927), gave birth to a golden era of power and the attendant bulging stadia.

When 1968 rolled around, "The Year of the Pitcher" was invasively thrust upon the baseball world. Bob Gibson's microscopic 1.12 ERA was an eye-popping performance and hitters were so befuddled only one American Leaguer hit .300. Baseball's response to the pendulum swing precipitously going the pitchers' way was the lowering of the mound. Since then virtually every significant rule change has favored hitters.

Hitters come in all shapes and sizes and their talents range from slugging with unbridled sheer power (think Ruth and Jimmie Foxx of long ago and big David Ortiz and Albert Pujols of today) to guiding the ball through and over holes with diamond-cutter precision à la Wee Willie Keeler, Paul Waner, Rod Carew, Wade Boggs, and Tony Gwynn.

Hitters and Hitting

The litany of hitters we loved to watch could fill a tome, a Pantheon—for that matter, a Hall of Fame. Like Stevie Wonder in his song *Sir Duke*, which paid tribute to a slew of marvelous singers, we too can rattle off the names of our heroes: the Georgia Peach, the Sultan of Swat, Double-X, the Rajah, Hammerin' Hank, the Mick, and Charlie Hustle.

No doubt about it, fans not only cherish the game's hitting stars, they also love to hear what hitters have to say.

● ● ●

"I keep a mental book on what pitchers throw me. When I'm hitting well, I can tell what a pitch will be when it's halfway to the plate."
—HANK AARON, BRAVES SUPERSTAR

• • •

"When I hit a ball, I want someone else to go chase it."
—HALL OF FAMER ROGERS HORNSBY ON WHY HE DIDN'T PLAY GOLF

• • •

"I'd rather try hitting a hummingbird than a knuckleball."
—HITTING GREAT PETE ROSE

• • •

"Once [Stan] Musial timed your fastball, your infielders were in jeopardy."
—PITCHING GREAT WARREN SPAHN

• • •

"Every great batter works on the theory that the pitcher is more afraid of him than he is of the pitcher."
—TIGER SUPERSTAR TY COBB

• • •

"You dumb hitters. By the time you know what to do, you're too old to do it."
—OUTFIELDER TED WILLIAMS

• • •

"There's a conspiracy among the clubs. Nobody's hiring
thirty-seven-year-old players who can't hit."
—FIRST BASEMAN MIKE JORGENSEN

• • •

"Most slumps are like the common cold. They last two weeks no
matter what you do."
—CATCHER TERRY KENNEDY

• • •

"Nobody should hit .200. Anybody should [be able to] hit .250."
—HITTING INSTRUCTOR CHARLIE LAU

• • •

"I wasn't in a slump. I just wasn't getting any hits."
—OUTFIELDER DAVE HENDERSON

• • •

"Hitting is 50 percent above the shoulders."
—HALL OF FAMER TED WILLIAMS

• • •

"You know you're going bad when your wife takes you aside and
tries to change your batting stance. And you take her advice."
—WRITER THOMAS BOSWELL, FROM *HOW LIFE
IMITATES THE WORLD SERIES*

• • •

"There is only one legitimate trick to pinch hitting and that's knowing the pitcher's best pitch when the count is 3-and-2. All the rest is a crapshoot."
—MANAGER EARL WEAVER

• • •

"I'd rather hit home runs. You don't have to run as hard."
—METS FIRST BASEMAN DAVE KINGMAN

• • •

"No one can ever see the ball hit the bat because it's physically impossible to focus your eyes that way. However, when I hit the ball especially hard, I could smell the leather start to burn as it struck the wooden bat."
—HALL OF FAMER TED WILLIAMS, FROM *OUT-OF-LEFT-FIELD BASEBALL TRIVIA* BY ROBERT OBOJSKI AND WAYNE STEWART

• • •

"We weren't a very subtle team. We didn't pull a lot of squeeze plays. All we tried to do was hit the ball so hard it broke in half."
—BOBBY BROWN, YANKEES THIRD BASEMAN, FROM *THE ERA* BY ROGER KAHN

• • •

"You guys are trying to stop [Stan] Musial in fifteen minutes when the National [League] ain't stopped him in fifteen years."
—CATCHER YOGI BERRA TO HIS PITCHERS AT AN ALL-STAR GAME

• • •

"George Brett could get wood on an aspirin."
—ROYALS MANAGER JIM FREY

• • •

"If I'm hitting, I can hit anyone. If not, my twelve-year-old son can get me out."
—PIRATES OUTFIELDER WILLIE STARGELL

• • •

"I get a kick out of watching a team defense me. A player moves two steps in one direction and I hit it two steps the other way. It goes right by his glove and I laugh."
—HITTING SENSATION ROD CAREW

• • •

"He [Harmon Killebrew] hit line drives that put the opposition in jeopardy. And I don't mean infielders, I mean outfielders."
—WASHINGTON SENATORS FARM DIRECTOR OSSIE BLUEGE

• • •

"I would think I drive most hitting coaches crazy. During one single at-bat I used six different stances on six pitches. Oh yeah, I also struck out. So what do I know?"
—OUTFIELDER JOHN KRUK

• • •

"So I'm ugly. So what? I never saw anyone hit with his face."
—YOGI BERRA, HALL OF FAME CATCHER

• • •

"You will never become a .300 hitter unless you take the bat off your shoulder."
—PITCHER CHIEF BENDER

• • •

"My favorite play is the hit and run. See who's covering [the bag] and hit a ground ball where he was."
—BATTING CHAMP TONY GWYNN

• • •

"He was something like 0-for-21 the first time I saw him. His first major league hit was a home run off me and I'll never forgive myself. We might have gotten rid of Willie [Mays] forever if I'd only struck him out."
—BRAVES GREAT WARREN SPAHN

• • •

"When a guy hits a really long home run, there's a completely different sound. Then everybody stops. You look up and see the ball up there in the crowd with the hot dog vendors. The popcorn goes flying. The beer goes flying. It's a sweet thing."
—HITTING COACH TOM MCCRAW

• • •

"He's the only player in baseball who consistently hits my grease. He sees the ball so well, I guess he can pick out the dry side."
—PITCHER GAYLORD PERRY ON ROD CAREW

• • •

"You have to swing like a man. A walk won't get you off the island."
—SHORTSTOP RAFAEL RAMIREZ ADDRESSING THE SUBJECT OF WHY PLAYERS FROM THE DOMINICAN REPUBLIC DREW SO FEW WALKS

• • •

"There are two theories on hitting the knuckleball. Unfortunately, neither of them works."
—HITTING INSTRUCTOR CHARLIE LAU

• • •

"I don't think God cares that we're not hitting. If he did, then Billy Graham would be hitting .400."
—REDS INFIELDER CHRIS SABO WHEN ASKED IF PRAYER MIGHT HELP

• • •

"Happiness is going 2-for-5 and seeing your average drop."
—THIRD BASEMAN RICHIE HEBNER

• • •

"You hit a four-ounce baseball with a thirty-five-ounce bat and there's going to be some damage."
—OUTFIELDER GEORGE FOSTER

• • •

"I see three baseballs, but I only swing at the middle one."
—PIRATE GREAT PAUL WANER ON HITTING AFTER A NIGHT OUT ON THE TOWN

• • •

"Your bat is your life. It's your weapon. You don't want to go into battle with anything that feels less than perfect."
—OUTFIELDER LOU BROCK

• • •

"As far as I'm concerned, there is no greater pleasure in the world than walking up to the plate with men on base and knowing that you are feared."
—CATCHER TED SIMMONS

• • •

"Young man, when you pitch a strike, Mr. [Rogers] Hornsby will let you know."
—UMPIRE BILL KLEM TO A ROOKIE PITCHER

• • •

"Mike [Piazza] turns mistakes into misery."
—ATLANTA PITCHER JOHN SMOLTZ, FROM *THE HISTORY OF THE NEW YORK METS* BY MICHAEL E. GOODMAN

• • •

"How can you hit and think at the same time?"
—CATCHER YOGI BERRA

• • •

"If I just hit the fastball hard, it tells me I can handle his velocity that night. It also gives the pitcher the same thought."
—LONGBALL HITTER MIKE SCHMIDT

• • •

"They're like sleeping in a soft bed. Easy to get into and hard to get out of."
—STAR CATCHER JOHNNY BENCH ON SLUMPS

• • •

"My motto was always to keep swinging. Whether I was in a slump or feeling badly or having trouble off the field, the only thing to do was keep swinging."
—HALL OF FAME OUTFIELDER HANK AARON

• • •

"It was an insurance run, so I hit it to the Prudential building."
—POWER HITTER REGGIE JACKSON

• • •

"I don't like to sound egotistical, but every time I stepped up to the plate with a bat in my hands, I couldn't help but feel sorry for the pitcher."
—HALL OF FAMER ROGERS HORNSBY

• • •

"The greatest thrill in the world is to end the game with a home run and watch everybody else walk off the field while you're running the bases on air."
—AL ROSEN, CLEVELAND INDIANS GREAT

• • •

"I'm up there with a bat and all the pitcher's got is the ball. I figure that makes it all in my favor. I let the fellow with the ball do the fretting."
—HALL OF FAMER HANK AARON

• • •

"I never saw anything like it. He doesn't just hit pitchers. He takes away their dignity."
—DODGER HALL OF FAMER DON SUTTON ON PIRATE SLUGGER WILLIE STARGELL

• • •

"Players from both teams watch when Bo [Jackson] takes batting practice. There's always the feeling that you're going to see something you never saw before and we don't want to miss it."
—BRET SABERHAGEN, PITCHER AND ROYALS TEAMMATE OF SLUGGER BO JACKSON

• • •

"With all the glamour attached to hitting the ball out of the park, it takes a lot of discipline to go up there and just try to get a base hit."
—OUTFIELDER GARRY MADDOX

• • •

"Don't forget to swing hard, in case you hit the ball."
—CLEVELAND INFIELDER WOODIE HELD

• • •

"The secret of hitting is physical relaxation, mental concentration—and don't hit the fly ball to center."
—ST. LOUIS GREAT STAN MUSIAL

PART FIVE

• • •

Pitchers and Pitching

Hitting aside, it is absolutely true that pitching is not only the name of the game, it is, according to experts such as the venerable Connie Mack, about "75 percent of baseball," and some place the percentage even higher. Good pitching has also been said to be so bedazzling that it can (and often does) simply over-power hitting. To use a baseball cliché, "Good pitching will always stop good hitting." Forget, for this chapter, another version of that quote that, after the words "good hitting," added the paradoxical phrase, "and vice versa."

It's hard to imagine now, in this age of 100-mph fastballs blazing downhill from the likes of 6'10" Randy Johnson, but origi-nally, by rule, a pitcher was in many ways a mere underhand lobber of offerings, not unlike slow-pitch softball pitchers. Further, there was a time when pitchers were required to, again, *by rule*, throw the ball either high or low as directed *by the batter*. Imagine, say, Albert Pujols being permitted to shout out a decree to the mound,

"I'd like another juicy pitch, say, belt high this time, thank you," with the pitcher having to comply!

After the turn of the century, the craft of pitching began to resemble what we've become accustomed to, as the stars came out. Early luminaries included Walter Johnson, Christy Mathewson, Grover Cleveland Alexander, and even George Herman Ruth. Nearly a full century later, today's fans are entertained by the modern men of the mound—you've got Greg Maddux, Roger Clemens, Mariano Rivera, et al.

Some pitchers' careers have been as ephemeral as the life of a mayfly (fittingly, also known as the "dayfly"). Cases in point: Minor league pitcher Stan Musial, who wound up pitching to just one batter at the big league level. Then there were Smoky Joe Wood, who lasted only about seven full seasons and then, due to an arm injury, became an outfielder; obscure Hall of Famer Addie Joss, who experienced only seven years with thirty or more starts and who died two days after his thirty-first birthday; and even Sandy Koufax, whose lifetime record stood at a mediocre 54-53 entering the 1962 season—he then rattled off a streak of five superlative seasons in which he led the league in ERA and tossed no-hitters seemingly effortlessly before bowing out prematurely at the age of thirty-one.

Conversely, other pitchers have lasted for decades, allowing us to savor their mastery endlessly; Nolan Ryan and Clemens epitomize that kind of rare hurler.

Many of the quotes in this chapter pay homage to laser-like fastballs, relying heavily on hyperbole. Pirates announcer Bob Prince, for instance, spoke not only of pitchers who threw BBs and of fastballs that could penetrate a sturdy wall, but he took it one step beyond and regaled listeners with tales of men who could fire a *strawberry* through a brick wall. Other quotes deal with crafty pitchers, with the strategy of pitching, and so on.

Clearly, pitching is a colorful part of the game, a crucial key to victories. Likewise, quotations on pitching are often illuminating, amusing, and "winning" as well.

• • •

"A pitcher pitches low instead of high because how often have you seen a 420-foot ground ball?"
—PITCHER JIM BUNNING

• • •

"Pitchers, like poets, are born, not made."
—CY YOUNG, WINNER OF A RECORD 511 BIG LEAGUE GAMES

• • •

"You haven't become a good pitcher until you can win when you don't have anything."
—PITCHER SANDY KOUFAX

• • •

"I knew I was in trouble when they started clocking my fastball with a sundial."
—PITCHER JOE MAGRANE

• • •

"I threw the ball so hard I tore a couple of boards off the grandstand. One of the fellows said that the stand looked like a cyclone struck it. That's how I got the name and it was shortened to Cy."
—PITCHING GREAT CY YOUNG

• • •

"Home plate is seventeen inches wide, but I ignore the middle twelve. I pitch to the two and a half inches on each side."
—PITCHING GREAT WARREN SPAHN

• • •

"We developed a very scientific system for bringing in relief pitchers. We used the first one who answered the telephone."
—PITCHING COACH CHUCK ESTRADA

• • •

"You gotta keep the ball off the fat part of the bat."
—PITCHER SATCHEL PAIGE

• • •

"Can I throw harder than Joe Wood? Listen, mister, no man alive can throw any harder than 'Smoky' Joe Wood."
—HALL OF FAME PITCHER WALTER JOHNSON

• • •

"Blind people come to the park just to listen to him pitch."
—SLUGGER REGGIE JACKSON ON TOM SEAVER

• • •

"I felt like shouting out that I had made a ball curve. I wanted to tell everybody; it was too good to keep to myself."
—PITCHER CANDY CUMMINGS, CREDITED AS THE FIRST PLAYER TO DISCOVER AND THROW A CURVE

• • •

"If they knocked one of our guys down, I'd knock down two of theirs. If they knocked two of our guys down, I'd get four. You have to protect your hitters."
—DODGERS GREAT DON DRYSDALE

• • •

"Pitching is essentially a sequential process that requires thinking like a hitter."
—PITCHING COACH ROGER CRAIG

• • •

"Nobody likes to hear it, because it's dull. But the reason you win or lose is darn near always the same—pitching."
—ORIOLES MANAGER EARL WEAVER

• • •

"Every hitter likes fastballs, just like everybody likes ice cream. But you don't like it when someone's stuffing it into you by the gallon."
—POWER HITTER REGGIE JACKSON ON TRYING TO HIT NOLAN RYAN'S FASTBALL

• • •

"My manager spent ten years trying to teach me a change of pace. At the end of my career that's all I had."
—PITCHER LEFTY GOMEZ

• • •

"A man should always hold something in reserve, a surprise to spring when things get tight."
—PITCHER CHRISTY MATHEWSON

• • •

"I'd pace myself. If I had a lead, I'd ease up. Then you can bear down on tough guys or save yourself for the next game. I didn't care about ERA, but it takes time to learn this. The bottom line is did you win or lose."
—CLEVELAND'S BOB FELLER, FROM *INDIANS ON THE GAME* BY WAYNE STEWART

• • •

"His fastballs sawed off bats at the top."
—PITCHER DIZZY DEAN ON SATCHEL PAIGE

• • •

"You can't be thinking about too many things. Relief pitchers have to get into a zone of their own."
—ROYALS RELIEVER DAN QUISENBERRY

• • •

"Trying to hit Phil Niekro is like trying to eat Jell-O with chopsticks. Once in a while you might get a piece, but most of the time you go hungry."
—OUTFIELDER BOBBY MURCER

• • •

"The most important things are location and knowing how to pitch. If you can't do those things up here, you can't win. It's as simple as that. You can forget about good stuff and you can forget about radar guns. If you can't locate your pitches, you can't win. Period."
—MANAGER LOU PINIELLA

• • •

"I hit guys in the ribs. The ribs don't move."
—INTIMIDATING PITCHER BOB GIBSON

• • •

"Any pitcher who's been around Greg Maddux and doesn't get it doesn't impress me."
—CARDINALS PITCHER JASON MARQUIS, FROM *USA TODAY*

• • •

"I just figured if the resin bag is out there, you're supposed to use it."
—PITCHER GAYLORD PERRY, WHO USED IT TO DEVISE HIS PUFF BALL, A PITCH THAT EMERGED OUT OF A PULL OF SMOKE

• • •

"Pitching, to me, is throwing strikes and throwing strikes down low. To be able to throw a fastball on the inside part of the plate and then on the outside part of the plate, within a range of two or three inches—that's big league control."
—METS ACE TOM SEAVER, FROM *THE HISTORY OF THE NEW YORK METS* BY MICHAEL E. GOODMAN

• • •

"Pitching is really just an internal struggle between the pitcher and his stuff. If my curve ball is breaking and I'm throwing it where I want, then the batter is irrelevant."
—CY YOUNG AWARD–WINNER STEVE STONE

• • •

"Without the deception of the curve, baseball would have become just another sport for young men of premium size and strength."
—WRITER MARTIN QUIGLEY

• • •

"A guy who throws what he intends to throw—that's the definition of a good pitcher."
—HALL OF FAME PITCHER SANDY KOUFAX

• • •

"I lost twenty-four games my first year with the Mets, you've got to be a pretty good pitcher to lose that many. What manager is going to let you go out there that often?"
—PITCHER ROGER CRAIG

• • •

"Hitters always have the fear that one pitch might get away from him and they'll wind up DOA with a tag on their toe."
—PITCHER RUDY MAY ON GOOSE GOSSAGE

• • •

"I throw as hard as I can when I think I have to throw as hard as I can."
—PITCHER WALTER JOHNSON

• • •

"He's baseball's exorcist—he scares the devil out of you."
—DETROIT OUTFIELDER DICK SHARON ON NOLAN
RYAN

• • •

"Throw high risers at the chin; throw peas at the knees; throw
it here when they're lookin' there; throw it there when they're
lookin' here."
—PITCHING LEGEND SATCHEL PAIGE

• • •

"A pitcher needs two pitches—one they're looking for and one to
cross them up."
—WARREN SPAHN, WINNINGEST LEFTY EVER

• • •

"There is no doubt that someone who tries to throw a curve or
pitch at an early age, before he's developed, before his hand is big
enough to grip the ball correctly, will damage his arm."
—HALL OF FAME PITCHER ROBIN ROBERTS

• • •

"It's not easy, but I trust my pitches and I trust my teammates
behind me."
—YANKEES CLOSER MARIANO RIVERA

• • •

"Natural grass is a wonderful thing for little bugs and sinkerball pitchers."
—RELIEVER DAN QUISENBERRY

• • •

"Trying to hit him was like trying to drink coffee with a fork."
—SLUGGER WILLIE STARGELL ON FACING
SOUTHPAW SANDY KOUFAX

• • •

"There is nothing quite like the feeling of expectation on the morning of the day or night that you are scheduled to pitch."
—HALL OF FAMER TOM SEAVER

• • •

"In my era, you've got Roger Clemens, Randy Johnson, Greg Maddux—but as far as I'm concerned, Pedro's the best."
—PITCHER BRET SABERHAGEN ON PEDRO
MARTINEZ, FROM *THE HISTORY OF THE BOSTON
RED SOX* BY AARON FRISCH

• • •

"They've got a lot of names for pitches now, but there are only so many ways you can throw a baseball."
—PETE REISER, AS A CUBS COACH

• • •

"He could thread a needle with that ball."
—LES BELL, INFIELDER, ON GROVER CLEVELAND
ALEXANDER

• • •

"You can't have a miracle every day—except you can when you
get great pitching."
—MANAGER CASEY STENGEL

• • •

"That's like asking if I'd rather be hung or go to the
electric chair."
—BALTIMORE'S MERV RETTENMUND, WHEN ASKED
IF HE'D RATHER HIT AGAINST TOM SEAVER OR JIM
PALMER

• • •

"The space between the white lines—that's my office. That's where
I conduct my business."
—INTIMIDATING PITCHER EARLY WYNN

• • •

"I hated to bat against [Don] Drysdale. After he hit you, he'd
come around, look at the bruise on your arm and say, 'Do you
want me to sign it?'"
—YANKEES GREAT MICKEY MANTLE

• • •

"What's the use of doing in three pitches what you can do in one."
—PITCHING GREAT GROVER CLEVELAND ALEXANDER, MINIMIZING THE IMPORTANCE OF STRIKE OUTS

• • •

"I became a good pitcher when I stopped trying to make them miss the ball and started trying to make them hit it."
—DODGERS GREAT SANDY KOUFAX

• • •

"I exploit the greed of all hitters."
—BRAVES STAR PITCHER LEW BURDETTE

• • •

"Whitey [Ford] was a master. It was like watching a pitching textbook in the flesh."
—YANKEES PITCHER RALPH TERRY

• • •

"Mother was a hell of a hitter."
—PITCHER EARLY WYNN ON BEING LABELED A PITCHER WHO "WOULDN'T GIVE HIS MOTHER A GOOD PITCH TO HIT."

• • •

"Hitting is timing. Pitching is upsetting timing."
—WARREN SPAHN, HALL OF FAME HURLER

• • •

"It actually giggles at you as it goes by."
—OUTFIELDER RICK MONDAY ON PHIL NIEKRO'S KNUCKLEBALL

• • •

"Everybody who pitches, pitches with some pain. . . . I would throw a pitch and it would hurt, but then the pain would go away—until the next pitch."
—CARDINALS GREAT BOB GIBSON

• • •

"A pitcher has to look at the hitter as his mortal enemy."
—EARLY WYNN, PITCHER FAMOUS FOR HIS FIERY TEMPER

• • •

"The owners think if I wasn't in baseball I'd be out digging ditches or something. That really fries me. How can they be in baseball and not see what it's all about? Pitching is a beautiful thing. It's an art."
—HALL OF FAMER TOM SEAVER

• • •

"I can see how he won twenty-five games. What I don't understand is how he lost five."
—ALL-STAR CATCHER YOGI BERRA ON DODGER GREAT SANDY KOUFAX'S STELLAR 1963 SEASON

• • •

"An elevated game of catch."
—PITCHING COACH RAY MILLER'S DEFINITION OF
PITCHING, FROM *BASEBALL DIGEST,* SEPTEMBER
1990

• • •

"The pitcher is the happiest with his arm idle. He prefers to
dawdle in the present, knowing that as soon as he gets on the
mound and starts his windup he delivers himself to the
uncertainty of the future."
—AUTHOR GEORGE PLIMPTON, FROM *OUT OF MY
LEAGUE*

• • •

"It was like talking to Thomas Edison about light bulbs."
—KNUCKLEBALL PITCHER TOM CANDIOTTI ON
HAVING THE OPPORTUNITY TO ASK KNUCKLEBALL
ARTIST PHIL NIEKRO FOR ADVICE

• • •

"People who write about spring training not being necessary have
never tried to throw a baseball."
—HALL OF FAMER SANDY KOUFAX

• • •

PART SIX

Stars and Superstars

ere you will find some of the words spoken by and about the true superstars of the game, as well as men who are lesser stars, but legitimately fine players nevertheless.

I've interviewed players since 1978 and I've found that frequently the most willing subjects and often the most interesting ones are not the stars, but marginal players. However, that said, some of my favorite interviewees were astute, incisive, and articulate men such as Tony Gwynn, Doug Drabek, Merv Rettenmund, Lee Smith, and Dale Murphy, all of them stars or superstars by anyone's definition.

So, while great quotations *can* come from virtually any baseball player, it's also true that most fans would much rather hear what the big stars have to say. When Vida Blue was a rookie back in 1971, he burst upon the baseball scene with the speed and force of a meteor. It didn't take him long to catch on to the fickle ways of the world. As he summed up, "It's a weird scene. You win a few baseball games and all of a sudden you're surrounded by reporters and TV men with cameras asking you about Vietnam and race relations."

Pete Rose, not a huge man, but one whose bulging forearms begged not for a tattoo of a battleship, but of an entire armada, is far from being a well-educated man, but when the subject is baseball, people pay heed—and that's quite natural. So natural that we've devoted an entire chapter to comments from the mouths of the game's luminaries. Not all of the quotations are exactly earth shattering, but hopefully they are of note.

The rostrum is loaded with men such as Ted Williams and Ty Cobb, fierce .400 hitters; Hank Aaron and Reggie Jackson, both laden with power; and men from as far back as "Shoeless" Joe Jackson and from players as recent as Johnny Damon.

So it's time now to listen to the words of and about men with split-second timing with the bat and precise hand-eye coordination. These are the men who made a name for themselves in the world of baseball, the stars and the superstars.

● ● ●

"I don't care to be known as a .400 hitter with a lousy average of .39955."
—BOSTON LEGEND TED WILLIAMS ON HIS REFUSAL TO SIT OUT A SEASON-ENDING DOUBLE HEADER TO PRESERVE HIS MATHEMATICALLY ROUNDED-UP-TO .400 AVERAGE IN 1941

• • •

"Hey, big mouth, how do you spell triple?"
—OUTFIELDER "SHOELESS" JOE JACKSON AFTER TRIPLING, TO A FAN WHO HAD HECKLED HIM EARLIER BY SHOUTING TO THE POORLY EDUCATED JACKSON, "HOW DO YOU SPELL ILLITERATE?"

• • •

"By accident he'll hit 35-40 home runs in our ballpark."
—MANAGER LEO DUROCHER ON WHY HE WANTED TO ACQUIRE SUPERSTAR FRANK ROBINSON, FROM *NICE GUYS FINISH LAST* BY LEO DUROCHER AND ED LINN

• • •

"When he [Rickey Henderson] came around, there wasn't anybody like him. He definitely was a trendsetter and he's what teams are looking for in a leadoff hitter. Before [him], leadoff hitters were just slap hitters and guys who could run very fast, but Rickey added the power to that game."
—OUTFIELDER JOHNNY DAMON, FROM *HITTING SECRETS OF THE PROS* BY WAYNE STEWART

• • •

"He's the kind of guy you'd like to kill if he's playing for the other team, but you'd take ten of him on your side."
—GENERAL MANAGER FRANK LANE OF BILLY MARTIN

• • •

"It's a weird scene. You win a few baseball games and all of a sudden you're surrounded by reporters and TV men with cameras asking you about Vietnam and race relations."
—ROOKIE PITCHING SENSATION VIDA BLUE IN 1971

• • •

"Stealing bases is like jumping out of a car that's going twenty miles per hour."
—SPEEDSTER WILLIE WILSON OF THE ROYALS

• • •

"I've got a hitch in my swing and I hit off the wrong foot. I've done it the wrong way my whole career."
—BRAVES IMMORTAL HANK AARON

• • •

"I always say, the only time you gotta worry about getting booed is when you're wearing a white [home] uniform. And I've never been booed wearing a white uniform."
—BATTING CHAMP PETE ROSE, FROM *THE PHILADELPHIA INQUIRER* (STORY BY ROSE), REPRINTED IN *THE COMPLETE ARMCHAIR BOOK OF BASEBALL,* EDITED BY JOHN THORN

• • •

"[Mickey] Mantle is the only man I ever saw who was crippled who could outdo the world."
—MANAGER CASEY STENGEL

• • •

"What all of this [Cal Ripken Jr.'s streak of games played in a row] is about is a man going to work every day to do his job."
—ORIOLES COACH CAL RIPKEN, SR., FROM *AND THE FANS ROARED* BY JOE GARNER

• • •

"If I had as many singles as Pete Rose, I'd have worn a dress."
—OUTFIELDER MICKEY MANTLE

• • •

"Does Pete [Rose] hustle? Before the All-Star game he came into the clubhouse and took off his shoes—and they ran another mile without him."
—ALL-TIME GREAT HANK AARON

• • •

"Ain't no man can avoid being born average, but there ain't no man got to be common."
—STAR PITCHER SATCHEL PAIGE

• • •

"When Joe [DiMaggio] came into the clubhouse it was like a senator or a president coming in."
—YANKEES INFIELDER BILLY MARTIN

• • •

"He looked like he was falling apart when he ran. Looked like he was coming apart when he threw. His stance at the plate was ridiculous . . . The only thing that made him look sensational was the results."
—PITCHER ROBIN ROBERTS ON ROBERTO CLEMENTE

• • •

"I've been calling big-league games for forty years and I can't remember anybody capturing the imaginations of the fans quite like this kid."
—CUBS ANNOUNCER HARRY CARAY ON RYNE SANDBERG

• • •

"Take Ted Williams—after all he did to the fans in Boston. He spat on them, gave them the obscene and vulgar gesture and, Christ, he hits a home run and they all stand up and cheer. You can't boo a home run."
—QUOTE FROM WRITER SHIRLEY POVICH, FROM *NO CHEERING IN THE PRESS BOX,* RECORDED AND EDITED BY JEROME HOLTZMAN

• • •

"[Lou] Gehrig never learned that a ballplayer couldn't be good every day."
—CATCHER HANK GOWDY

• • •

"Robin [Yount] had so much ability, we just had to let him play. He was just a baby out there, but you could see early on that he'd be a great one."
—YOUNT'S FIRST BIG LEAGUE MANAGER, DEL CRANDALL, FROM *THE HISTORY OF THE MILWAUKEE BREWERS* BY RICHARD RAMBECK

• • •

"Big Papi [David Ortiz] is an action superhero come to life."
—*BOSTON GLOBE* WRITER DAN SHAUGHNESSY, FROM *BASEBALL DIGEST,* DECEMBER 2006

• • •

"Back when I came up, baseball was about establishing yourself. You wanted to get into a position to break the records of the players you grew up watching."
—PADRES HITTING SENSATION TONY GWYNN

• • •

"The big trouble is not really who isn't in the Hall of Fame, but who is. It was established for a select few."
—HALL OF FAMER ROGERS HORNSBY

• • •

"When Ty's Southern blood is aroused he is a bad man to handle."
—MANAGER HUGH JENNINGS ON COBB

• • •

"They hung the nickname 'The Commerce Comet' on him, except he was faster than a comet. Fastest thing I ever saw."
—YANKEES PITCHER TOM STURDIVANT ON MICKEY MANTLE

• • •

"He [track star Carl Lewis] makes his living running fast and I make mine running slow."
—POWER HITTER BARRY BONDS ON HIS DELIBERATE HOME RUN TROT

• • •

"A chunky, unshaven hobo who ran the bases like a berserk loco-motive, slept in the raw and swore at pitchers in his sleep."
—AUTHOR LEE ALLEN ON PEPPER MARTIN, FROM HIS BOOK *THE NATIONAL LEAGUE*

• • •

"One time in the car I asked him [Hank Aaron] why he never talked about hitting . . . I'll never forget what he said. He said, 'If you can do it, you don't have to talk about it.'"
—BRAVES PUBLICITY DIRECTOR BOB ALLEN, FROM *I HAD A HAMMER* BY HANK AARON WITH LONNIE WHEELER

• • •

"Everybody in the park knows he's going to run [steal] and he makes it anyway."
—SHORTSTOP LARRY BOWA ON LOU BROCK

• • •

"Just as nature fills a vacuum, Reggie [Jackson] fills a spotlight."
—AUTHOR BOB MARSHALL

• • •

"Batting against Don Drysdale is the same as making a date with the dentist."
—SHORTSTOP DICK GROAT

• • •

"Old Detroit [Tigers Stadium] with [memories of] Ty Cobb and Boston with [the tradition of] Ted Williams and Carl Yastrzemski—I really enjoy knowing that you're playing on the same field with all the greats."
—YANKEES STAR DON MATTINGLY ON SOME OF THE OLD PARKS HE LOVED TO PLAY IN

• • •

"That's what you do in the postseason; you get it to 'Mo.' You start checking off the innings and try to get him into the ballgame."
—YANKEES JASON GIAMBI ON MARIANO RIVERA

• • •

"He [Pete Rose] gets base hits in the present and lives in the past. He should be dancing the Charleston, drinking sarsaparilla and wearing a big-brimmed fedora."
—WRITER LARRY MERCHANT, FROM HIS BOOK *RINGSIDE SEAT AT THE CIRCUS*

• • •

"This team, it all flows from me. I've got to keep it going. I'm the straw that stirs the drink."
—YANKEES REGGIE JACKSON

• • •

"I've never heard a bat louder than his. You hear it going through the strike zone and the sound is unmistakable. It goes 'Vump.' That's when he misses."
—RED SOX ANNOUNCER KEN HARRELSON ON JIM RICE

• • •

"I was raised, but I never did grow up."
—SUPERSTAR PETE ROSE

• • •

"Such golden creatures—a young Willie Mays, say—are awesome to observe but not especially rewarding as a subject for study: one can take apart a watch but not a sunset."
—AUTHOR ROGER ANGELL, FROM HIS BOOK *LATE INNINGS*

• • •

"Check Donnie's eyes out during a game. They're right out of a horror movie. He yells at opposing players. He paces the dugout. I've never seen anyone compete with that kind of passion."
—YANKEES PITCHER BOB TEWKSBURY ON TEAMMATE DON MATTINGLY, FROM *THE HISTORY OF THE NEW YORK YANKEES* BY MICHAEL E. GOODMAN

• • •

"He [Rogers Hornsby] was frank to the point of being cruel and subtle as a belch."
—WRITER LEE ALLEN

• • •

"He plays like he's on a mini-trampoline out there or wearing
helium kangaroo shorts maybe."
—OUTFIELDER ANDY VAN SLYKE ON OZZIE SMITH

• • •

"There were days when Mickey Mantle was so darn good that we
kids would bet that even God would want his autograph."
—ANNOUNCER BOB COSTAS

• • •

"[Willie] Wilson has unreal speed. He's a walking double."
—OUTFIELDER REGGIE JACKSON

• • •

"You grab hold of him and it's like grabbing hold of steel."
—CUBS MANAGER BOB SCHEFFING ON HIS STAR
PLAYER ERNIE BANKS

• • •

"I'm no different from anyone else with two legs and 4,200 hits."
—HIT KING PETE ROSE

• • •

"I had to fight all my life to survive. They were all against me . . .
but I beat the bastards and left them in the ditch."
—FORMER ALL-TIME HIT KING TY COBB

• • •

"You're not always going to come through. There's been plenty of times that I haven't. But when I'm in that [key] situation, I feel as though I'm going to produce . . ."
—YANKEES STAR DEREK JETER

● ● ●

"The bigger the guy, the less he argues. You never heard a word out of Stan Musial or Willie Mays or Roberto Clemente. They never tried to make you look bad."
—VETERAN UMPIRE TOM GORMAN

● ● ●

"If I can change the score, I'm not going to worry about getting hurt."
—AGGRESSIVE BASE RUNNER PETE ROSE

● ● ●

"[Greg Maddux's] kind of talent usually comes with an ego sidecar. He doesn't have it. He's as easygoing as the guy next door."
—BRAVES GENERAL MANAGER JOHN SCHUERHOLTZ

● ● ●

"Walk by a house that's being built, stop awhile and watch the bricklayers. Pretty soon you'll be able to tell who is the best brick-layer by his drive, his determination. Pete [Rose] has more drive within him. He's the best bricklayer out there."
—PIRATES STAR WILLIE STARGELL

● ● ●

"If they ever let him play in a small place like Ebbets Field or old Fenway Park, Josh Gibson would have forced baseball to rewrite the rules. He was, at the minimum, two Yogi Berras."
—TEAM OWNER BILL VEECK

• • •

"I don't think anybody has ever been that good at that age [nineteen]. He's in his own category."
—MARINERS HITTING COACH GENE CLINES ON KEN GRIFFEY, JR., FROM *THE HISTORY OF THE SEATTLE MARINERS* BY MICHAEL E. GOODMAN

• • •

"We have three leagues now. There's the American, the National, and there's Ted Williams."
—RED SOX PITCHER MICKEY HARRIS

• • •

"This game is too much fun to ever get too old to play it."
—PITCHER TUG MCGRAW

• • •

"I have the greatest job in the world."
—YANKEES SHORTSTOP DEREK JETER

• • •

"There's no scouting report on handling Albert Pujols. 'Don't even try,' the [unnamed] scout says."
—QUOTE FROM *USA TODAY* PRIOR TO 2006 PLAYOFFS

• • •

"Show me a guy who's afraid to look bad and I'll show you a guy you can beat every time."
—HALL OF FAMER LOU BROCK

• • •

"If my uniform doesn't get dirty, I haven't done anything in the baseball game."
—STAR OUTFIELDER RICKEY HENDERSON

• • •

"Because I wanted to win the game."
—OUTFIELDER ROGER MARIS WHEN ASKED WHY HE BUNTED RATHER THAN WENT FOR THE FENCES

• • •

"To play ball was all I lived for."
—YANKEE OUTFIELDER MICKEY MANTLE

• • •

"I've found that you don't need to wear a necktie if you can hit."
—BOSTON GREAT TED WILLIAMS

• • •

"I wasn't going to walk him. That wouldn't have been fair to him or me. Hell, he's the greatest player I ever saw."
—ST. LOUIS BROWNS PITCHER BOB MUNCRIEF, WHO HAD THE CHANCE TO STOP JOE DIMAGGIO'S HITTING STREAK AT 35, BUT CHALLENGED HIM AND SURRENDERED A SINGLE IN DIMAGGIO'S LAST AT BAT OF THE GAME

• • •

"Brooks [Robinson] never asked anyone to name a candy bar after him. In Baltimore, people name their children after him."
—SPORTSWRITER GORDON BEARD

• • •

"A foul ball was a moral victory."
—PITCHER DON SUTTON ON SANDY KOUFAX

• • •

"Too many people think an athlete's life can be an open book. You're supposed to be an example. Why do I have to be an example for your kid? You be an example for your kid."
—PITCHING ACE BOB GIBSON

• • •

"It's like crying for your mother after she's gone. You cry because you love her. I cried, I guess, because I loved baseball and I knew I had to leave it."
—ALL-TIME GREAT WILLIE MAYS, THEN WITH THE METS

• • •

"During my eighteen years I came to bat almost 10,000 times. I struck out about 1,700 times and walked maybe 1,800 times. You figure a ballplayer will average about 500 at bats a season. That means I played seven years in the major leagues without even hitting the ball."
—YANKEE GREAT MICKEY MANTLE

• • •

"I really thought they [Stan Musial, Ted Williams, and Jackie Robinson] put their pants on different, rather than one leg at a time."
—SUPERSTAR HANK AARON

• • •

"I ain't never had a job. I just always played baseball."
—PITCHER SATCHEL PAIGE

• • •

"If the human body recognized agony and frustration, people would never run marathons, have babies, or play baseball."
—CATCHER CARLTON FISK

• • •

"Here stands baseball's perfect warrior. Here stands baseball's perfect knight."
—BASEBALL COMMISSIONER FORD FRICK ON ST. LOUIS SUPERSTAR STAN MUSIAL

• • •

"He was sometimes unbearable, but he was never dull."
—BIOGRAPHER ED LINN ON TED WILLIAMS

• • •

"The ballplayer who loses his head, who can't keep his cool, is
worse than no ballplayer at all."
—YANKEES LEGEND LOU GEHRIG

• • •

"A homer a day will boost my pay."
—NEGRO LEAGUE LEGEND JOSH GIBSON

• • •

"There have been only two geniuses in the world. Willie Mays
and William Shakespeare."
—ACTRESS TALLULAH BANKHEAD

• • •

"Home run hitters drive Cadillacs. Singles hitters drive Fords."
—SLUGGER RALPH KINER

• • •

"People ask me what I do in winter when there's no baseball. I'll
tell you what I do. I stare out the window and wait for spring."
—HALL OF FAMER ROGERS HORNSBY

• • •

"He's a terrific guy and the world's quietest person. The night he broke [Lou] Gehrig's record, he went out and painted the town beige."
—BILLY RIPKEN, UTILITY MAN, ON HIS BROTHER CAL

• • •

"When you're eight games behind, it's like eight miles; when you're eight games in front, it's like eight inches."
—CUBS STAR THIRD BASEMAN RON SANTO

• • •

"You must have an alibi to show why you lost. If you haven't one, you must fake one. Your self-confidence must be maintained. Always have an alibi. But keep it to yourself. That's where it belongs."
—CHRISTY MATHEWSON, PITCHING GREAT

• • •

"You look for his weakness and while you're looking for it, he's liable to hit forty-five home runs."
—PITCHER SATCHEL PAIGE ON JOSH GIBSON

• • •

"I never perceived myself to be the big star. I'm only one of nine guys. I think it is good to think that way."
—BALTIMORE LEGEND CAL RIPKEN, JR.

• • •

"Every time I look at my pocketbook, I see Jackie Robinson."
—HALL OF FAMER WILLIE MAYS

• • •

"I loved the game. I loved the competition. But I never had any fun. I never enjoyed it. All hard work, all the time."
—BOSTON GREAT CARL YASTRZEMSKI

• • •

"I'm always going to have trouble saying [Willie] Mays, [Stan] Musial, and Morgan in the same breath."
—SECOND BASEMAN JOE MORGAN UPON HIS HALL OF FAME INDUCTION

• • •

"It's a great accomplishment to blend power with consistency. When I was playing in the league, he was the only one I considered a true superstar."
—HALL OF FAMER FRANK ROBINSON ON BOSTON'S CARL YASTRZEMSKI, FROM *THE HISTORY OF THE BOSTON RED SOX* BY RICHARD RAMBECK

• • •

"He walks like a crab, fields like an octopus, and hits like the devil."
—UNIDENTIFIED SPORTSWRITER ON HONUS WAGNER, PITTSBURGH'S LEGENDARY SHORTSTOP

• • •

"There are only two places in this league. First place
and no place."
—PITCHING GREAT TOM SEAVER

• • •

"Who wants to play in a game that means nothing?"
—OUTFIELDER ROBERTO CLEMENTE

• • •

"There's no pressure here. This is a lot of fun. Pressure is when
you have to go to the unemployment office to pick up a check to
support four people."
—ROYALS STAR GEORGE BRETT

• • •

"He's the nearest thing to a perfect ballplayer."
—BASEBALL LEGEND TY COBB ON HALL OF FAMER
GEORGE SISLER

• • •

"I want to thank the good Lord for making me a Yankee."
—CENTER FIELDER JOE DIMAGGIO

• • •

"I want to be remembered as a ballplayer who gave all he
had to give."
—PIRATES GREAT ROBERTO CLEMENTE

• • •

"Either he throws the fastest ball I've ever seen, or I'm going blind."
—OUTFIELDER RICHIE ASHBURN ON SANDY KOUFAX

• • •

"I was a little nervous out there. It was like any opening day. I don't care how long you played—you always get a little nervous."
—CATCHING GREAT YOGI BERRA

• • •

"[Ty] Cobb lived off the field as though he wished to live forever. He lived on the field as though it was his last day."
—BASEBALL EXECUTIVE BRANCH RICKEY

• • •

"I'll take any way to get into the Hall of Fame. If they want a batboy, I'll go in as a batboy."
—YANKEES INFIELDER PHIL RIZZUTO

• • •

"When you call a pitcher 'Lefty' and everybody in both leagues knows who you mean, he must be pretty good."
—ROYALS OUTFIELDER CLINT HURDLE ON PHILLIES ACE STEVE CARLTON

• • •

"I don't want them to forget Ruth. I just want them to remember me."
—HANK AARON, ALL-TIME HOME RUN KING

• • •

"Spahn and Sain, then pray for rain."
—WIDELY QUOTED OF BRAVES STAR PITCHERS
WARREN SPAHN AND JOHNNY SAIN

• • •

"You talk about a role model, this is a role model: Don't be like me. God gave me the ability to play baseball and I wasted it."
—HALL OF FAMER MICKEY MANTLE

• • •

"When I began playing the game, baseball was about as gentlemanly as a kick in the crotch."
—HALL OF FAME OUTFIELDER TY COBB

• • •

"Somebody's gotta win and somebody's gotta lose—and I believe in letting the other guy lose."
—BATTING CHAMP PETE ROSE

• • •

PART SEVEN

Fielding and Fielders

When it comes to the defensive side of the game, there are, as is the case with hitting and pitching, many fine quotes to be found. However, in this case, the quotations frequently tend to run to two extremes—there are the words of praise and hyperbole employed to describe the great gloves and then there are the words of humor and even derision to describe not the gold, but the iron gloves. It's a case of beauty and the butcher.

Therefore, this chapter, of course, includes kudos for the Ozzie Smiths, Johnny Benches, and Brooks Robinsons of baseball. After all, dazzling glovework elicits 4th of July "ooohs" and "ahhhs" from the grandstand. So tribute must also be paid to Roberto Clemente, Willie Mays, et al.

On the other hand, this chapter is also peppered with comments about the men such as Babe Herman and Jose Canseco who share the ignominy of having fly balls ricochet off their heads—capers such as theirs evoke laugher and incredulity but should also be chronicled. For instance, in my book, *Baseball Oddities*, I wrote that on Canseco's strangest defensive close encounter with a baseball he "resembled a combination of a ballerina and a soccer player as he first pirouetted back on the ball before he 'headed' it. That is to say he actually had the ball bounce off his noggin and over the wall for perhaps the most bizarre home run ever." That misadventure prompted Cleveland's general manager John Hart to mutter, "In my life I've never seen anything like that. I was stunned. I've seen balls hit outfielders on the head before, but not one that bounced over the fence." And, when reporters asked Texas infielder Julio Franco if he had ever seen such an odd play, he simply said, "Yeah, in a cartoon."

So, thanks to blooper films, fans can delight in zany misplays, perhaps taking solace that even big leaguers can botch a play or two. "Why, I coulda caught *that* ball," a fan might boast, no doubt deluding himself. Further, thanks to the vast media coverage of the game nowadays and special features such as Web Gems, fans can also marvel at the athleticism of contemporary glove magicians.

Therefore, from gloves that go "clank" to the gloves of gold, here's the opportunity to take a look and a figurative listen to quotations involving fielders and the act of fielding.

• • •

"Two-thirds of the earth is covered by water. The other one-third is covered by Garry Maddox."
—RALPH KINER, ANNOUNCER, ON OUTFIELDER GARRY MADDOX

• • •

"I bet he couldn't make that play again, not even on instant replay."
—SECOND SACKER RED SCHOENDIENST OF OUTFIELDER ROBERTO CLEMENTE, ALSO ATTRIBUTED TO OTHERS (E.G. BILL VIRDON ON LOU BROCK)

• • •

"When I throw a ground ball, I expect it to be an out—maybe two."
—PITCHER WARREN SPAHN

• • •

"My best pitch is anything the batter grounds, lines, or pops in the direction of Phil Rizzuto."
—YANKEE PITCHER VIC RASCHI ON HIS TEAMMATE

• • •

"I think defense belongs in the Hall of Fame. Defense deserves as much credit as pitching and hitting and I'm proud to be going in as a defensive player."
—SECOND BASEMAN BILL MAZEROSKI, FROM *MORE TALES FROM THE DUGOUT* BY MIKE SHANNON

• • •

"The phrase 'off with the crack of the bat,' while romantic, is really meaningless, since the outfielder should be in motion long before he hears the sound of the ball meeting the bat."
—CENTER FIELDER JOE DIMAGGIO

• • •

"He [Roberto Clemente] had that great arm, but I really don't understand how it held up, because when we'd take infield he'd throw like the game depended on it."
—PIRATES OUTFIELDER BILL VIRDON, FROM *TALES FROM THE BALLPARK* BY MIKE SHANNON

• • •

"The minute his glove touches the ball, it's out of his hands and on the way either to the infield or the plate. I've never seen a man get the ball back into play so fast."
—CUBS MANAGER STAN HACK ON WILLIE MAYS

• • •

"Jorge Orta never got acquainted with his glove, never met a ground ball he liked."
—WHITE SOX EXECUTIVE PAUL RICHARDS

• • •

"His [Roberto Clemente's] throws combined strength, accuracy, and speed of release in whatever proportions were necessary to get the job done."
—AUTHOR BILL JAMES, FROM HIS BOOK *THE BILL JAMES HISTORICAL BASEBALL ABSTRACT*

• • •

"By the end of the season I felt like a used car."
—CATCHER BOB BRENLY

• • •

"If I stay healthy, I have a chance to become the first player ever
to collect 3,000 hits and 1,000 errors."
—THIRD BASEMAN GEORGE BRETT

• • •

"I think being able to play the infield, especially shortstop, is
something you're born with. You can't learn it."
—STANDOUT SHORTSTOP DAVE CONCEPCION

• • •

"I fought the wall and the wall won."
—OUTFIELDER DMITRI YOUNG AFTER CRASHING
INTO THE WALL IN PURSUIT OF A FLY BALL

• • •

"It was his solemn duty to catch a ball that wasn't in the stands."
—OUTFIELDER MONTE IRVIN ON HIS GIANTS
TEAMMATE WILLIE MAYS

• • •

"Having [Randy] Hundley catch for you was like sitting down to
a steak dinner with a steak knife. Without Hundley all you had
was a fork."
—CUBS PITCHING GREAT FERGIE JENKINS

• • •

"That isn't an arm, that's a rifle."
—OAKLAND CATCHER GENE TENACE ON JOHNNY
BENCH'S ARM

• • •

"What was I supposed to say? Glad you got over Watergate?"
—SECOND BASEMAN STEVE SAX, REGARDING
FORMER PRESIDENT NIXON'S HAVING COMMENTED
HE WAS GLAD SAX OVERCAME HIS THROWING
DIFFICULTIES

• • •

"The catcher is the physical and emotional focus of every baseball
game; he faces outward, surveying and guiding it all and everyone else on the team looks in at him."
—AUTHOR ROGER ANGELL, FROM *LATE INNINGS*

• • •

"Defense is baseball's visible poetry and its invisible virtue."
—WRITER THOMAS BOSWELL

• • •

"[Bill Terry] concentrated entirely on defense. His theory was not
to let the other club score and they'd beat themselves."
—MANAGER PAUL RICHARDS

• • •

"Look, I like hitting fourth and I like the good batting average. But what I do every day behind the plate is a lot more important because it touches so many more people and so many more aspects of the game."
—YANKEES CATCHER THURMAN MUNSON

• • •

"The best way to catch a knuckleball is to wait until the ball stops rolling and then pick it up."
—CATCHER BOB UECKER

• • •

"He fields better on one leg than anybody else I got on two."
—METS MANAGER CASEY STENGEL OF HIS FIRST BASEMAN GIL HODGES

• • •

"There isn't anything to the pivot [on a double play], if you have guts enough to stand there."
—INFIELDER ROD KANEHL, FROM *THE JOCKS* BY LEONARD SHECTER

• • •

"If you're doing a quality job [as the catcher], you should almost be anonymous."
—CATCHER BOB BOONE

• • •

"If a woman has to choose between catching a fly ball and saving an infant's life, she will choose to save the infant's life without even considering if there are men on base."
—HUMORIST DAVE BARRY

• • •

"I was out there mowing the lawn during the [players'] strike. I got the front yard done and half the backyard and I kept waiting for Sam Mejias to come out and finish it for me."
—REDS OUTFIELDER DAVE COLLINS, ACCUSTOMED TO BEING YANKED FOR DEFENSIVE PURPOSES LATE IN GAMES

• • •

"The secret of my success was clean living and a fast-moving outfield."
—LEFTY GOMEZ, HALL OF FAME PITCHER

• • •

"Don't hit it to me."
—OUTFIELDER JOSE CANSECO WHEN ASKED HOW HIS TEAM COULD IMPROVE DEFENSIVELY

• • •

"There are some fielders who make the impossible catch look ordinary and some the ordinary catch look impossible."
—MANAGER JOE MCCARTHY

• • •

"I'd rather have a Gold Glove than a Silver Slugger. Defense is so much more of a team game."
—INFIELDER ALEX RODRIGUEZ

• • •

"Luis Aparicio is the only guy that I ever saw go behind second base, make the turn, and throw Mickey Mantle out. He was as sure-handed as anyone."
—YANKEE INFIELDER PHIL RIZZUTO

• • •

"I was a pudgy kid. That [catcher's position] was the only place for me to play."
—ALL-TIME GREAT JOSH GIBSON

• • •

"I tried to jump as high as I can, but I knew I had like a 10 percent chance in my mind that I could catch it. I improvised and did it on the run. See the ball. See the wall. Do the thing that I've got to do."
—METS OUTFIELDER ENDY CHAVEZ ON HIS GREAT LEAPING CATCH IN GAME 7 OF THE 2006 NLCS

• • •

"They want me to play third like Brooks Robinson, but I think I play it more like Mel Brooks."
—PADRES INFIELDER TIM FLANNERY

• • •

"He's a Williams type player. He bats like Ted and fields like Esther."
—NEWSPAPER ITEM ON FIRST BASEMAN DICK STUART

• • •

"You start chasing a ball and your brain immediately commands your body to, 'Run forward! Bend! Scoop up the ball! Peg it to the infield! Then your body says, 'Who, me?'"
—YANKEE OUTFIELDER JOE DIMAGGIO ON AGING FIELDERS

• • •

"Don't get me wrong, I like to hit. But there's nothing like getting out there in the outfield, running after a ball and throwing somebody out trying to take that extra base. That's real fun."
—CENTERFIELD SENSATION WILLIE MAYS, FROM THE *SPORTING NEWS*

• • •

"I never had to be lonely behind the plate, where I could talk to the hitters. I also learned that by engaging them in conversation I could sometimes distract them."
—CATCHING GREAT ROY CAMPANELLA

• • •

Fielding and Fielders

"Pop flies, in a sense, are just a diversion for a second baseman. Grounders are his stock in trade."
—INFIELDER JACKIE ROBINSON

• • •

"When a fielder gets a pitcher in trouble, the pitcher has to pitch himself out of a slump he isn't in."
—MANAGER CASEY STENGEL

• • •

"A catcher and his body are like the outlaw and his horse. He's got to ride that nag till it drops."
—HALL OF FAME CATCHER JOHNNY BENCH

• • •

"If you prefer baseball in slow motion, don't miss George Foster chasing a double into the leftfield corner."
—SPORTSWRITER CHARLES BRICKER

• • •

"There's nothing tough about playing third. All a guy needs is a strong arm and a strong chest."
—PIRATES MANAGER FRANKIE FRISCH

• • •

"It's a pretty sure thing that the player's bat is what speaks loudest when it's contract time, but there are moments when the glove has the last word."
—THIRD BASEMAN BROOKS ROBINSON

• • •

"I don't like them fellas who drive in two runs and let in three."
—MANAGER CASEY STENGEL

• • •

"God watches over drunks and third basemen."
—LEO DUROCHER, MANAGER

• • •

"Why should I go jack-knifing over the fence on my head? That
ball has got no business being out there 400 feet."
—OUTFIELDER REGGIE SMITH

• • •

"I don't compare them, I just catch them."
—CENTER FIELDER WILLIE MAYS WHEN ASKED
HOW HIS 1954 WORLD SERIES CLASSIC CATCH
RANKED AMONG HIS BEST EVER

• • •

"A great catch is like watching girls go by. The last one you see is
always the prettiest."
—PITCHER BOB GIBSON

• • •

"Good defense in baseball is like good umpiring: It's there, you
expect it, but you don't really appreciate it. But when it isn't there,
then you notice it."
—INFIELDER DOUG DECINCES

• • •

"Willie Mays' glove is where triples go to die."
—SPORTSWRITER JIM MURRAY, ALSO ATTRIBUTED
TO ANNOUNCER VIN SCULLY, AND TO FRESCO
THOMPSON AS "WILLIE MAYS AND HIS GLOVE:
WHERE TRIPLES GO TO DIE."

• • •

"The only way I'm going to get a Gold Glove is with a can of
spray paint."
—SLUGGER REGGIE JACKSON

• • •

"The way to get a hit past Honus [Wagner] is to hit it eight feet
over his head."
—MANAGER JOHN MCGRAW

• • •

"He can play all three outfield positions—at the same time."
—MANAGER GENE MAUCH OF HOUSTON'S CESAR
CEDENO

• • •

"He reacted to the ball with the speed of a sedated hippo."
—SPORTSWRITER LOWELL COHN ON GIANTS
OUTFIELDER JACK CLARK

• • •

"Errors are a part of the game, but Abner Doubleday was a jerk for inventing them."
—JOURNEYMAN BILLY RIPKEN

• • •

"Never once did I get hit on the head by a fly ball. Once or twice on the shoulder maybe, but never on the head."
—BABE HERMAN, DEFENDING HIS TERRIBLE DEFENSE

• • •

"Defense does make pitching, but the defense doesn't have to be sensational. If they just make the routine plays, that's all you want. Spectacular plays are overrated."
—METS MANAGER GEORGE BAMBERGER

• • •

"If the ball went up, I know I must catch it. This was for the enjoyment of the people who came out to see me play."
—CENTER FIELDER WILLIE MAYS, FROM *WILLIE'S TIME* BY CHARLES EINSTEIN

• • •

"Get in front of those balls; you won't get hurt. That's what you've got a chest for, young man."
—GIANTS MANAGER JOHN MCGRAW

• • •

PART EIGHT

Managers and Managing

I t's a very exclusive club, the circle of men who run big league teams. After all, at any given time there are only thirty human beings on the face of the planet who hold the occupation of big league manager—even though the hold on that title is often quite tenuous. Their job description and duties run the gamut from the handling of men (many of them temperamental with colossal egos), to dealing with a global and ever more demanding media, to actually doing what managers almost universally say they love doing the most and which they actually find to be the easiest part of their job: the running of the team on the field, the guiding their players through games, constantly making split-second decisions, and playing that baseball/chess game of planning several innings ahead.

The men who have held down this job have come from diverse backgrounds. Bob Boone, for instance, holds a degree in psychology, yet contends that hasn't really helped him as a manager. "I don't think there's a direct correlation . . . it's not like, 'Gee, you went to Stanford and you have a degree in psychology, therefore you're an expert and you can psychoanalyze everybody.' I think that's completely a farce . . ."

Meanwhile, many managers of the early days of baseball were far from being well educated; some never even finished high school. Casey Stengel may have been called the Old Professor, but listening to him for just a few seconds would reveal he was hardly a scholar.

Of course, men such as Stengel were, in a baseball sense, quite cerebral (see Warren Spahn's more fitting take on Stengel in this chapter). Luckily, too, many managers possess a wonderful sense of humor (necessary when combating the tribulations of their job), sometimes sharp and sarcastic, other times self-deprecating and, best of all, often just downright hilarious.

So, it's time to delve into the world of minor and major league managers and to take in the humor as well as the insights their words reveal.

• • •

"Hold them for a few innings, fellas. I'll think of something."
—CONFIDENT MANAGER CHARLIE DRESSEN, ALSO
ATTRIBUTED TO JOHN MCGRAW

• • •

"Aren't all managers interim?"
—ORIOLES PITCHER MIKE FLANAGAN

• • •

"The rules are made by me, but I don't have to follow them."
—MANAGER BILLY MARTIN

• • •

"He's no Boy Scout, but he understands people. You'll get no
special favors from him, but neither will anybody else."
—GIANTS OUTFIELDER MONTE IRVIN ON LEO
DUROCHER

• • •

"Gene Mauch's stare can put you on the disabled list."
—CATCHER TIM MCCARVER

• • •

"You only win with talent."
—MANAGER SPARKY ANDERSON

• • •

"There are only two things a manager needs to know: when to change pitchers and how to get along with your players."
—SENATORS MANAGER BUCKY HARRIS

• • •

"We could finish first or in an asylum."
—FRANKIE FRISCH, MANAGER OF THE GASHOUSE GANG

• • •

"One place I won't allow my players to drink is at the hotel where we're staying. That's where I do my drinking."
—MANAGER CASEY STENGEL, ALSO ATTRIBUTED TO A'S MANAGER HANK BAUER

• • •

"You gotta lose 'em sometime. When you do, lose 'em right."
—MANAGER CASEY STENGEL

• • •

"The greatest feeling in the world is to win a major league game. The second-greatest feeling is to lose a major league game."
—MANAGER CHUCK TANNER

• • •

"He would play a convicted rapist if he could turn the double play."
—PITCHER JIM BOUTON ON MANAGER LEO DUROCHER

• • •

"Because you can't fire the entire team."
—RED SOX GENERAL MANAGER DICK O'CONNELL ON WHY HE FIRED MANAGER DARRELL JOHNSON

• • •

"You couldn't fool Casey [Stengel] because he'd pulled every stunt that ever was thought up and he did it fifty years before we even got there."
—YANKEE GREAT MICKEY MANTLE

• • •

"They're [managers] a necessary evil. I don't believe a manager ever won a pennant. Casey Stengel won all those pennants with the Yankees. How many did he win with the Boston Braves and Mets?"
—MANAGER SPARKY ANDERSON

• • •

"If you do the screaming, the players won't. If you get thrown out, they won't. You've got to keep the players in the lineup."
—EARL WEAVER, ORIOLES MANAGER

• • •

"I think we can win it—if my brains hold out."
—GIANTS MANAGER JOHN MCGRAW IN THE THICK
OF A PENNANT RACE

• • •

"I'm not one of those old-timers who say everything was better in
my day. I think ballplayers today are better than the players were
when I played. But what ever happened to 'sit down, shut up, and
listen'?"
—LEO DUROCHER, LONG-TIME BIG LEAGUE
MANAGER

• • •

"You never unpack your suitcase in this business."
—MANAGER PRESTON GOMEZ UPON BEING FIRED

• • •

"I think there should be bad blood between all clubs."
—ORIOLES MANAGER EARL WEAVER

• • •

"Never give up on a player until you know whom you're going to
replace him with."
—FROM *THE BILL JAMES GUIDE TO BASEBALL
MANAGERS* BY BILL JAMES

• • •

"I'm Billy's best friend and even I don't like him."
—PITCHER WHITEY FORD JOKING ABOUT BILLY
MARTIN

• • •

"There has been only one manager and his name is John
McGraw."
—LEGENDARY MANAGER CONNIE MACK ON A
FELLOW LEGEND, FROM *THE HISTORY OF THE SAN
FRANCISCO GIANTS* BY AARON FRISCH

• • •

"In the thirteen years I managed in the big leagues,
they [umpires] must have made a million calls—and
they were wrong just ninety-one times."
—EARL WEAVER, ORIOLES MANAGER, ALLUDING
TO THE NINETY-ONE TIMES HE WAS KICKED OUT
OF GAMES

• • •

"When fans come to the ballpark, damn it, every last one of them
is a manager."
—WHITEY HERZOG, LONG-TIME SKIPPER

• • •

"Managing is not running, hitting, stealing. Managing is getting
your players to put out 100 percent year after year."
—REDS MANAGER SPARKY ANDERSON

• • •

"It's better to lose a game by making a move than lose it sitting on my ass."
—ORIOLES MANAGER EARL WEAVER, FROM HIS BOOK *WINNING!*

• • •

"Listen, if you start worrying about the people in the stands, before too long you're up in the stands with them."
—DODGER MANAGER TOMMY LASORDA

• • •

"I don't throw the first punch. I throw the second four."
—A'S MANAGER BILLY MARTIN

• • •

"You don't worry about injuries this time of year. We're in a pennant race. If you can walk, you can play."
—METS MANAGER DAVEY JOHNSON

• • •

"Losing streaks are funny. If you lose at the beginning, you get off to a bad start. If you lose in the middle of the season, you're in a slump. If you lose at the end, you're choking."
—MANAGER GENE MAUCH, WHOSE 1964 PHILLIES FOLDED DOWN THE STRETCH

• • •

"You argue with an umpire because there's nothing else you can do about it."
—MANAGER LEO DUROCHER

• • •

"If you want job security, drive a mail truck."
—ALVIN DARK, GIANTS SKIPPER

• • •

"Say you were standing with one foot in the oven and one foot in an ice bucket. According to percentage people, you should be perfectly comfortable."
—MANAGER BOBBY BRAGAN

• • •

"Managing is getting paid for home runs someone else hits."
—HALL OF FAMER CASEY STENGEL

• • •

"I've always said I could manage Adolph Hitler, Benito Mussolini, and Hirohito. That doesn't mean I'd like them, but I'd manage them."
—YANKEES SKIPPER BILLY MARTIN

• • •

"If you ain't got a bullpen, you ain't got nothin'."
—MANAGER YOGI BERRA

• • •

"Don't find many faults with the umpire. You can't expect him to be as perfect as you are."
—YANKEES MANAGER JOE MCCARTHY

• • •

"I don't want guys who just try hard. I tried hard and I didn't get out of A-ball."
—MANAGER JIM LEYLAND

• • •

"Sometimes I think I'm in the greatest business in the world. Then you lose four straight and want to change places with the farmer."
—YANKEES MANAGER JOE MCCARTHY

• • •

"Baseball has got to be fun, because if it's not fun, it's a long time to be in agony."
—MANAGER TOM TREBELHORN, FROM *MEN AT WORK* BY GEORGE F. WILL

• • •

"There are only two kinds of managers. Winning managers and ex-managers."
—GIL HODGES, METS MANAGER

• • •

"I don't give a damn about the color of a man's skin. I'm only interested in how well or how badly he plays this game."
—MANAGER LEO DUROCHER

• • •

"Being with a woman all night never hurt no professional baseball player. It's the staying up all night looking for one that does him in."
—MANAGER CASEY STENGEL

• • •

"You have to improve your club if it means letting your own brother go."
—JOE MCCARTHY, MANAGER OF THE YANKEES

• • •

"Tell a ballplayer something a thousand times. Then tell him again because that might be the time he'll understand something."
—MANAGER PAUL RICHARDS

• • •

"What do managers really do? Worry. Constantly. For a living."
—WRITER LEONARD KOPPETT, FROM *A THINKING MAN'S GUIDE TO BASEBALL*

• • •

"If you make a player feel like nothing, he'll play like nothing. I want them all coming to the park with the feeling that they have a chance to get in the game."
—ANGELS MANAGER GENE MAUCH

• • •

"We have deep depth."
—MANAGER YOGI BERRA

• • •

"I come to play. I come to beat you. I come to kill you."
—LEGENDARY MANAGER LEO DUROCHER

• • •

"The pilgrims didn't have any experience when they first arrived here. Hell, if experience was that important, we'd never have had anybody walking on the moon."
—MANAGERIAL CANDIDATE DOUG RADER

• • •

"There's no room for sentiment in baseball if you want to win."
—PLAYER-MANAGER FRANKIE FRISCH

• • •

"Everything looks nicer when you win. The girls are prettier. The cigars taste better. The trees are greener."
—MANGER BILLY MARTIN WAXING PHILOSOPHICALLY

• • •

"No matter how good you are, you're going to lose one-third of your games. No matter how bad you are, you're going to win one-third of your games. It's the other third that makes the difference."
—DODGER MANAGER TOMMY LASORDA

• • •

"They say some of my stars drink whiskey, but I have found that the ones who drink milkshakes don't win many ballgames."
—HALL OF FAMER CASEY STENGEL

• • •

"I'm probably the only guy who played for [Casey] Stengel before and after he was a genius."
—HALL OF FAMER WARREN SPAHN, WHO PLAYED UNDER STENGEL ON THE BOSTON BRAVES AND ON THE NEW YORK METS

• • •

"I never questioned the integrity of an umpire. Their eyesight, yes."
—HALL OF FAME MANAGER LEO DUROCHER

• • •

"In this game of baseball, you live by the sword and die by it. You hit and get hit. Remember that."
—ALVIN DARK, MANAGER OF THE INDIANS, ON KNOCKDOWN AND BRUSHBACK PITCHES

• • •

PART NINE

Keys to Success

Many books have been written on how to succeed in business and a series of books offering tips on various topics for "idiots" fills bookshelves across the nation. In baseball, too, there are entire tomes devoted to success. Subtopics include everything from hitting, pitching, and fielding fundamentals to how a front office puts together a winner and to how a successful manager runs a team. Culling many of the words of wisdom from books, players, managers, coaches, team owners, ad infinitum, here now are some important quotations on the keys to baseball success.

While everyone can spout the lines about the key to baseball being pitching and/or three-run homers, the comments below offer a veritable diamond seminar. Further, since the game is made up of so many facets, going beyond the generalities of pitching and power, this chapter touches on many more aspects of baseball, such as the art of base burglary. After all, one perks up his ears when, say, Maury Wills or Lou Brock speaks of larceny on the base paths.

Likewise, an aspiring hitter must pay heed to the likes of a Ted Williams when he spouts words of wisdom such as his idea of making sure one gets a good pitch to hit: "It means a ball that does not fool you, a ball that is not in a tough spot for you. Think of trying to hit it back up the middle. Try not to pull it every time."

Naturally, too, a pitching prospect listens aptly, *very* attentively, as a Bob Gibson speaks of his craft and how he had disdain for waste pitches: "On an 0-and-2 count, throw your best fastball or slider. Don't lay it in there when you've got 0-and-2 on the batter."

Some of the advice here is very general, as is true of Roger Clemens' terse "You have to strap it on and go get them." Other keys to success are quite specific, such as Tom Seaver's "The good rising fastball is the best pitch in baseball." Still other quotations are rather philosophical in nature; consider Earl Weaver's famous line, "It's what you learn after you know it all that counts." Ted Turner, former owner of the Atlanta Braves, once summed up his idea of what it takes to win thusly: "What you've got to have in baseball is pitching, speed, and money." Finally, some keys don't even pertain to on-the-field facets, but instead concern intangible facets of baseball. As pitcher Andy Messersmith once put it, "Championships are won in the clubhouse."

So, here now is a crash course on success in the game of baseball.

• • •

"Trade a player a year too early rather than a year too late."
—BASEBALL EXECUTIVE BRANCH RICKEY

• • •

"Winning isn't everything. Wanting to win is."
—PITCHER CATFISH HUNTER

• • •

"I was told by a very smart man a long time ago that talent always beats experience. Because by the time you get experience, the talent's gone."
—PHILADELPHIA PHILLIES MANAGER PAT CORRALES

• • •

"Be relaxed, don't wave the bat, don't clench it. Be ready to hit down with the barrel of the bat. Just swing it and let the weight drive the ball."
—PIRATES OUTFIELD GREAT PAUL WANER

• • •

"Success has no shortcut, only a high price of pain and humiliation. Baseball requires mental strength."
—CATCHER CARLTON FISK

• • •

"Never the same pitch twice, never the same place twice, never the same speed twice."
—PITCHER ED LOPAT'S TIPS ON PITCHING SUCCESS

• • •

"It's like most anything. If you want to be a loser, there's always a way to dwell on the negative. If you want to win, there's always a way to think positively."
—MANAGER TONY LA RUSSA

• • •

"Study and work at the game as if it were a science."
—TIP FROM HALL OF FAMER TY COBB

• • •

"A manager wins games in December. He tries not to lose them in July. You win pennants in the offseason when you build your team with trades and free agents."
—ORIOLES MANAGER EARL WEAVER

• • •

"Stand your ground and take your lumps."
—ADVICE OF CATCHER YOGI BERRA

• • •

"You hit home runs not by chance, but by preparation."
—YANKEE SLUGGER ROGER MARIS

• • •

"When you steal a base, 99 percent of the time you steal on a pitcher. You actually never steal on a catcher."
—FORMER STOLEN BASE KING LOU BROCK

• • •

"You would think that more pitchers would realize just how much they can help their winning average by their fielding ability."
—EDDIE YOST, INFIELDER

• • •

"Never swing at a ball you're fooled on or have trouble hitting."
—BATTING TIP FROM OUTFIELDER TED WILLIAMS

• • •

"Scouts would always tell me I was too short, or too heavy, or whatever. But baseball isn't about being a size or a shape. It's about how big you are inside that counts."
—TWINS STAR OUTFIELDER KIRBY PUCKETT
FROM *THE HISTORY OF THE MINNESOTA TWINS* BY
RICHARD RAMBECK

• • •

"Win any way you can, so long as you can get away with it."
—LEO DUROCHER, LONGTIME BIG LEAGUE
MANAGER

• • •

"It's a simple game. It's the same game that our dads and moms taught us in the backyards: 'Play! Catch the ball. See the ball. Hit it. Make a good throw.'"
—BALTIMORE COACH ELROD HENDRICKS

• • •

"Sweat plus sacrifice equals success."
—OAKLAND A'S OWNER CHARLIE FINLEY

• • •

"This game is built on adjustment—constant adjustment. Talent will take you so far. That's why you see guys do well for a couple of years and then drop out of sight. You have to be willing to adjust."
—MANAGER MIKE HARGROVE, FROM *BASEBALL DIGEST*, JULY 1994

• • •

"It helps if the hitter thinks you're a little crazy."
—HALL OF FAME PITCHER NOLAN RYAN, ALL-TIME STRIKEOUT KING

• • •

"Losing is no disgrace if you've given your best."
—HALL OF FAMER JIM PALMER

• • •

"I'm looking for a ballplayer with enough guts *not* to fight back."
—BROOKLYN EXECUTIVE BRANCH RICKEY ON THE
KEY TO JACKIE ROBINSON, SIGNED AS THE FIRST
AFRICAN-AMERICAN PLAYER, AFTER ROBINSON
HAD ASKED RICKEY IF HE WAS LOOKING FOR "A
NEGRO WHO IS AFRAID TO FIGHT BACK."

• • •

"After two strikes, concede the long ball to the pitcher; shorten up
on the bat and try to put the head of the bat on the ball."
—BOSTON'S SUPERSTAR TED WILLIAMS

• • •

"What you've got to have in baseball is pitching, speed, and
money."
—ATLANTA BRAVES OWNER TED TURNER

• • •

"You have to set the goals that are almost out of reach. If you set
a goal that is attainable without much work or thought, you are
stuck with something below your true talent and potential."
—FIRST BASEMAN STEVE GARVEY

• • •

"Under pressure, you want to be at peace with yourself.
You want your energy to flow, not feel knotted. You don't want
to be too sharp. You don't want to be too flat. You just want to be
natural."
—PIRATES SLUGGER WILLIE STARGELL

• • •

"You can't have dissension if you want to be in contention."
—REDS OUTFIELDER GEORGE FOSTER

• • •

"Many players are thrown out by a split second. When you hit the ball, run it out with all the speed you have, no matter where or how you hit it."
—OUTFIELDER TY COBB

• • •

"On an 0-and-2 count, throw your best fastball or slider. Don't lay it in there when you've got 0-and-2 on the batter."
—BOB GIBSON, ONE OF HIS KEYS TO SUCCESS

• • •

"[Hank] Greenberg made a great hitter out of himself. He did it by constant practice . . . He'd stay after games and hit until darkness made him quit."
—MANAGER PAUL RICHARD

• • •

"What does that [getting a good ball to hit] mean? It means a ball that does not fool you, a ball that is not in a tough spot for you. Think of trying to hit it back up the middle. Try not to pull it every time."
—OUTFIELDER TED WILLIAMS

• • •

"He had that fear that the great ones have. He had that fear of failure and I think he tried to minimize that possibility by working to make sure all margin for error was eliminated."
—CUBS MANAGER JIM FREY ON HALL OF FAMER RYNE SANDBERG

• • •

"They [big leaguers] know what they can do and what they cannot. To 'stay within yourself' is to keep your balance. A player's reach should not exceed his grasp."
—AUTHOR GEORGE F. WILL, FROM HIS BOOK *MEN AT WORK*

• • •

"You can learn little from victory. You can learn everything from defeat."
—HALL OF FAME PITCHER CHRISTY MATHEWSON

• • •

"Not relying on any one guy but getting contributions from every single person on the roster, that's how we win."
—SHORTSTOP DEREK JETER

• • •

"You have to strap it on and go get them."
—PITCHING SENSATION ROGER CLEMENS

• • •

"It is just as important to know when not to go [try to steal a base] as it is to know when to go."
—SPEEDSTER MAURY WILLS OF THE DODGERS

• • •

"Throw strikes. Home plate don't move."
—PITCHER SATCHEL PAIGE

• • •

"If you play an aggressive, hustling game, it forces your opponents into errors."
—PETE ROSE, ALL-TIME HIT KING

• • •

"It's what you learn after you know it all that counts."
—BALTIMORE MANAGER EARL WEAVER

• • •

"When you're a winner you're always happy, but if you're happy as a loser you'll always be a loser."
—COLORFUL TIGER PITCHER MARK FIDRYCH

• • •

"Winning depends on where you put your priorities. It's usually best to put them over the fence."
—SLUGGER JASON GIAMBI

• • •

"A good base stealer should make the whole infield jumpy.
Whether you steal or not, you're changing the rhythm of the
game."
—JOE MORGAN, HALL OF FAMER

• • •

"Twenty-five players, one heartbeat."
—FLORIDA MANAGER JIM LEYLAND ON WHAT IT
TAKES FOR SUCCESS

• • •

"If a man can beat you, walk him."
—LEGENDARY PITCHER SATCHEL PAIGE

• • •

"You gotta be a man to play baseball for a living, but you gotta
have a lot of little boy in you, too."
—THREE-TIME MVP ROY CAMPANELLA

• • •

"There's a certain scent when you get close to winning. You may
go a long time without winning, but you never forget that scent."
—KANSAS CITY PITCHER STEVE BUSBY

• • •

"In order to be an outstanding base runner, you have to eliminate
the fear of failure. It's like being a safecracker."
—DODGER SHORTSTOP MAURY WILLS

• • •

"Speed is a great asset; but it's greater when it's combined with quickness—and there's a big difference."
—TIGERS GREAT TY COBB

• • •

"Every time you learn something, it helps you—maybe a week, a month, maybe a year from now. Once you stop learning—let me tell you—you're going to be in the second row looking at somebody else playing."
—HALL OF FAME PITCHER FERGIE JENKINS

• • •

"Progress always involves risks. You can't steal second bases and keep your foot on first."
—WRITER FREDERICK B. WILCOX

• • •

"When I get to first I figure second and third will be mine in just a second or two."
—SPEEDY ROYALS OUTFIELDER WILLIE WILSON ON THE CONFIDENCE NEEDED TO SUCCEED

• • •

"[Batting] . . . is a study in psychology, a sizing up of pitcher and catcher and observing little details that are of immense importance."
—HALL OF FAMER TY COBB

• • •

PART TEN

The World Series

It has been called both the Fall and the Autumnal Classic and this series of crucial games, the true granddaddy of championship sporting events in the United States, has been around, uninterrupted save two times, since 1903 when the Pittsburgh Pirates lost to the Boston franchise then known as the Americans. The first contest of the event, also then called "The Championship of the United States," was held at Boston's Huntington Avenue Grounds, as was the finale, a game witnessed by only 7,455 fans. Back then, by the way, it was a best-of-nine series, and *this* Boston crew stormed back from a deficit of one win to Pittsburgh's three, taking the final four games, a bit like the back-to-the-wall Boston Red Sox of 2004 in their playoff versus the Yankees.

Some of the World Series have been duds and four-game sweeps tend to leave little room for dramatics. Fortunately, though, the pyrotechnics and the tension of moments such as Pittsburgh's win behind Bill Mazeroski's ultimate walk-off home run versus the Yanks in 1960 (or Joe Carter's three-run, Series-ending homer off

Mitch Williams for the Toronto Blue Jays in 1993) provide lasting thrills.

On the other side of the coin, the pitching realm, there have been classic match-ups such as the 1968 duel between Detroit Tigers Mickey Lolich and St. Louis Cardinals ace Bob Gibson. Both men entered the seventh game with a 2-0 slate and both threw shutout ball through the first six frames before Gibson blinked and Lolich, on two days' rest, won to become one of a handful of pitchers to nail down three Series games. Of course, the ultimate in pitching perfection for an entire Series (no disrespect meant for Don Larsen's perfect game in 1956) came way back in 1905 when Christy Mathewson of the New York Giants not only notched three wins, but did so by firing three shutouts. That's good for an invisible ERA of 0.00 over 27 innings with 18 K's (versus only one walk) to boot as he held the Philadelphia Athletics to an average of five base runners per game.

It's only natural, then, that this event has led to some great quotations as well. It's time now to relive those words.

• • •

The World Series

"I can't remember the last time I missed a ground ball. I'll remember that one."
—BOSTON'S BILL BUCKNER OF HIS INFAMOUS ERROR IN GAME 6 OF THE 1986 WORLD SERIES, ALLOWING THE BALL TO SCOOT THROUGH HIS LEGS AT FIRST BASE

• • •

"What does a mama bear on the pill have in common with the World Series? No cubs."
—CUBS ANNOUNCER HARRY CARAY

• • •

"If you do everything right, you'll still lose 40 percent of your games—but you'll also end up in the World Series."
—WRITER THOMAS BOSWELL

• • •

"We are part of history. We are something special. We were playing for more than the World Series. Now we have some bragging rights."
—YANKEES OUTFIELDER BERNIE WILLIAMS AFTER WINNING THE 2000 SERIES VERSUS CROSSTOWN RIVALS THE METS

• • •

"My Triple Crown season would have meant nothing, it would have been a waste, unless we got the world championship back."
—YANKEES GREAT MICKEY MANTLE

• • •

165

"That first World Series finished baseball as a sport. Afterwards the owners and later the ballplayers became big-time businessmen."
—SPORTSWRITER JOHN R. TUNIS, QUOTED IN *THE HEAD GAME* BY ROGER KAHN

• • •

"It's never happened in the World Series competition and it still hasn't."
—CATCHER YOGI BERRA ON DON LARSEN'S PERFECT GAME

• • •

"It's like the Fourth of July, New Year's Eve, and your birthday all wrapped in one."
—PITCHER TOM SEAVER ON THE FEEL OF THE WORLD SERIES

• • •

"I don't want to be one of those great players who never made the Series."
—OUTFIELDER RICKEY HENDERSON ON BEING TRADED TO THE YANKEES

• • •

"I don't think you play this game for any other reason than to get to the World Series. I've thought about it since Little League, when you dream of hitting that home run in the ninth inning."
—SLUGGER KEN GRIFFEY, JR.

• • •

"I had two great thrills in the World Series—when I thought it was over and then when it actually was over."
—PITCHER SANDY KOUFAX OF THE CLIMAX TO THE 1963 WORLD SERIES

• • •

"We are never too old or too bothered to see ourselves wrapping up a World Series victory with a homer in the final inning of the seventh game."
—WRITER RON FIMRITE

• • •

"Where else would you want to be in October, except here?"
—YANKEES SHORTSTOP DEREK JETER ON THE WORLD SERIES

• • •

"I guess the biggest thrill I had was crouching behind the plate, giving signals when Ted Williams was the hitter. I didn't know whether to call the pitch or get his autograph."
—CATCHER JOE GARAGIOLA OF THE CARDINALS ON THE WORLD SERIES OF 1946

• • •

"Even when your grandkids have grandkids, nobody will win it the way we did in '85 . . . That was a team that got pushed right up against the wall and, somehow, the wall moved."
—ROYALS THIRD BASEMAN GEORGE BRETT

• • •

"There is no script."
—CARDINALS MANAGER TONY LA RUSSA ON THE
UNPREDICTABILITY OF WORLD SERIES PLAY, FROM
THE ASSOCIATED PRESS

• • •

"You have to understand how difficult it is. There are so many
variables. You need talent, breaks, timing, and luck. You just try
not to set yourself up too high to get disappointed."
—CATCHER MIKE PIAZZA ON WINNING IN
POSTSEASON PLAY, FROM *USA TODAY*

• • •

"Baseball is really two sports—the summer game and the autumn
game. One is the leisurely pastime of our national mythology.
The other is not so gentle."
—WRITER THOMAS BOSWELL FROM *HOW LIFE
IMITATES THE WORLD SERIES*

• • •

"One day we were the laughingstock of baseball and the next we
were champions."
—FIRST BASEMAN ED KRANEPOOL OF HIS "MIRACLE
METS" OF '69

• • •

"The mark of a team isn't winning the championship; it's how you
defend the championship."
—YANKEES OWNER GEORGE STEINBRENNER

• • •

"Don't ask me how we did it—mirrors, magic wands, whatever. What does it matter? We did it!"
—METS OUTFIELDER MOOKIE WILSON ON CAPTURING THE 1986 WORLD SERIES, FROM *THE HISTORY OF THE NEW YORK METS* BY MICHAEL E. GOODMAN

• • •

"The balls aren't the same balls, the bats aren't the same length, and it's further between the bases."
—OUTFIELDER REGGIE JACKSON ON THE PRESSURE OF THE WORLD SERIES

• • •

"I would have needed a shotgun to get him out of the game."
—TWINS MANAGER TOM KELLY ON JACK MORRIS'S GRUELING 10-INNING VICTORY IN THE 1987 WORLD SERIES, FROM *THE HISTORY OF THE MINNESOTA TWINS* BY RICHARD RAMBECK

• • •

"I turned my back and ran, looked over my shoulder once to gauge the flight of the ball, then kept running. I caught it the way a football end catches a long leading pass. Then I spun and threw."
—GIANTS CENTER FIELDER WILLIE MAYS, RECAPPING HIS FAMOUS CATCH OF A DRIVE HIT BY VIC WERTZ IN THE 1954 WORLD SERIES

• • •

"Eighty-six years of 'waiting 'til next year,' and then to have it come to fruition, was something special, long beyond people's expectations."
—HALL OF FAME CATCHER CARLTON FISK ON THE RED SOX SERIES WIN IN 2004

• • •

"I must admit when Reggie Jackson hit that third home run [in a single World Series game] and I was sure nobody was listening, I applauded into my glove."
—STAR FIRST BASEMAN STEVE GARVEY, THEN WITH THE DODGERS

• • •

"The World Series is American sport's annual ticket to a romantic yesterday, when we all were young and surely going to be in the big leagues some day."
—WRITER RAY FITZGERALD, FROM *THE SPORTING NEWS*

• • •

"Baseball is a team game, but what Brooks did is as close as I've ever seen one player come to winning a series by himself."
—ORIOLES MANAGER EARL WEAVER ON BROOKS ROBINSON'S DAZZLING PLAY IN THE 1970 WORLD SERIES, FROM *THE HISTORY OF THE BALTIMORE ORIOLES* BY JOHN NICHOLS

• • •

"No matter how long you have been playing, you still get butterflies before the big one."
—BROOKLYN'S PEE WEE REESE ON THE WORLD SERIES

• • •

"It's the same as any other ballgame you'll remember as long as you live."
—CATCHER JOE GARAGIOLA ON WORLD SERIES PLAY

• • •

"When the astronauts walked on the moon I figured we had a chance to win. Nothing seemed impossible after that."
—RELIEF PITCHER TUG MCGRAW OF THE "MIRACLE METS" OF 1969

• • •

"October. That's when they pay off for playing ball."
—YANKEES OUTFIELDER REGGIE JACKSON

• • •

"No sports event in our history has consistently captured the hearts of the public as much as the World Series. Traditionally, it has been the ultimate in sports competition."
—BASEBALL COMMISSIONER BOWIE KUHN

• • •

"After seventeen major-league seasons, Roberto Clemente is an overnight sensation."
—SPORTSWRITER JERRY IZENBERG ON CLEMENTE'S SURGE IN FAME AFTER HIS 1971 SERIES HEROICS

• • •

"Not playing in a World Series for a great hitter is like not making the Met for a great singer, not playing the Old Vic for a great actor."
—SPORTSWRITER JIM MURRAY

• • •

"I think everybody was thinking we were going to say, 'Wait 'til next year' again. But here I was, just a kid from upstate New York and I beat the mighty Yankees. That's unheard of."
—DODGERS PITCHER JOHNNY PODRES ON KNOCKING OFF THE YANKS IN 1955, FROM *USA TODAY SPORTS WEEKLY*

• • •

PART ELEVEN

Wacky Quotes

Some of the quotes from the realm of baseball go beyond merely being funny; they border on the bizarre or the outrageous. In a sport packed with what were once called "flakes," it's only natural that baseball has produced some of the most unnatural quotes in all of sports.

Start with relievers, the facet of baseball so crucial to winning, so pressure-filled that one would think all relief pitchers (especially the notoriously zany lefties) must be just one bad outing away from the cardiac unit. Instead, many successful relievers have an equanimity with a devil-may-care sense of humor to match.

Larry Andersen was a cross between the one-line slinging Henny Youngman and the thought-provoking Steven Wright, and such a blend resulted in some of the wildest and funniest comments in baseball history.

Tug McGraw, father of country singer Tim, had a refreshing, unique take on the game. The southpaw reliever once wrote a fable whose protagonist was a baseball named Larry who had a dream to appear in a World Series. McGraw threw a screwball, at times was accused of being one, and even inspired and worked on a comic strip fittingly entitled "Scroogie."

Others pitchers such as Bill Lee came up with observations that left listeners wondering if Lee was a flake or a philosopher—of course, his nickname, "Spaceman," kind of skewed any such debate.

Like Lee, Jay Hanna Dean's nickname, Dizzy (his brother was Daffy), says it all, and boy, could he come up with some gems. Likewise, Satchel Paige could have authored his own version of Bartlett's book of quotations, baseball style. Like Steve Martin with Dan Aykroyd on the old *Saturday Night Live* skits, ol' Satch was one wild and crazy guy.

Baseball also produced colorful characters Casey Stengel and Yogi Berra, two men widely known for their non sequiturs that left fans laughing while scratching their heads. Sure, many quotes attributed to them were apocryphal—many, in fact, drummed up by writers—but they're still hilarious.

Toss in Graig Nettles, whose humor ranged from twisted to satiric, and Andy Van Slyke, who could have flourished doing a stand-up act. The list of baseball wits continues unabated and their quotes range from the offbeat to the enigmatic. Enjoy.

● ● ●

"You can only be young once, but you can be immature forever."
—RELIEF PITCHER LARRY ANDERSEN

• • •

"Ninety percent I'll spend on good times, women, and Irish whiskey. The other 10 percent I'll probably waste."
—RELIEF PITCHER TUG MCGRAW

• • •

"Something like four thousand bottles have been thrown at me in my day but only about twenty ever hit me. That does not speak very well for the accuracy of the fans' throwing."
—UMPIRE HARRY "STEAMBOAT" JOHNSON

• • •

"Most people are dead at my age."
—MANAGER CASEY STENGEL, UPON TURNING SEVENTY-FIVE

• • •

"The way to make coaches think you're in shape in the spring is to get a tan."
—YANKEES PITCHER WHITEY FORD

• • •

"The only thing running and exercising can do for you is make you healthy."
—PITCHER MICKEY LOLICH

• • •

"Tomorrow is another day. Unless you're not alive."
—WHITE SOX MANAGER TERRY BEVINGTON

• • •

"The highlight of your season is taking the team picture, knowing that the trading deadline has passed and you're a part of the club."
—EX-CATCHER JOE GARAGIOLA

• • •

"Why do people sing 'Take Me Out to the Ballgame' when they're already there?"
—RELIEF PITCHER LARRY ANDERSEN

• • •

"It's a beautiful day for a night game."
—FRANKIE FRISCH, AS AN ANNOUNCER

• • •

"I took a little English, a little math, some science, a few hubcaps, and some wheel covers."
—OUTFIELDER GATES BROWN OF HIS SHADY HIGH SCHOOL YEARS

• • •

"Now I won't be able to sign my letters 'Senator Henry Bonura, Democrat, Louisiana.'"
—ZEKE BONURA AFTER BEING SWAPPED FROM THE SENATORS

• • •

"Bill Buckner had a nineteen-game hitting streak going and always wore the same underwear. Of course, he didn't have any friends."
—INFIELDER LENNY RANDLE

• • •

"My only regret in life is that I can't sit in the stands and watch me pitch."
—ANGELS PITCHER BO BELINSKY, FROM *THE SUITORS OF SPRING* BY PAT JORDAN

• • •

"The wind, the fog rolling in . . . if that's not excitement enough, they ought to just plant land mines arbitrarily in the outfield."
—ST. LOUIS PITCHER JOE MAGRANE ON CANDLESTICK PARK IN SAN FRANCISCO

• • •

"Mike Anderson's limitations are limitless."
—PHILLIES MANAGER DANNY OZARK ON HIS OUTFIELDER

• • •

"If people don't want to come to the ballpark, how are you gonna stop them?"
—CATCHER YOGI BERRA

• • •

"When he [Darryl] Strawberry punched Keith Hernandez in spring training last season, it was the only time that Strawberry would hit the cutoff man all year."
—WRITER STEVE WULF

• • •

"It's tough to make predictions, especially about the future."
—CATCHER YOGI BERRA

• • •

"That's what I get for thinking on a baseball field."
—ALBERT BELLE, INDIANS OUTFIELDER, AFTER LOSING TRACK OF THE NUMBER OF OUTS

• • •

"Some people say you have to be crazy to be a reliever. Well, I don't know, I was crazy before I became one."
—PITCHER SPARKY LYLE

• • •

"I went through life as a 'player to be named later.'"
—CATCHER JOE GARAGIOLA

• • •

"So all those people booing wouldn't know you were my father."
—SPARKY ANDERSON'S DAUGHTER, SHIRLEE, AFTER HE ASKED HER WHY SHE HAD BOOED HIM

• • •

"During the years ahead, when you come to a fork in the road,
take it."
—YOGI BERRA, YANKEES CATCHER

● ● ●

"It's a lot easier when you're starting, because when you're
starting you can pick your days to drink."
—PITCHER BILL LEE ON HIS PREFERENCE TO BE A
STARTER RATHER THAN A RELIEVER

● ● ●

"You gotta have a catcher. If you don't have a catcher, you'll have a
lot of passed balls."
—METS SKIPPER CASEY STENGEL ON WHY HE
DRAFTED A CATCHER FIRST IN THE EXPANSION
DRAFT

● ● ●

"I've got a jackass back in Oklahoma and you can work with
him from sunup till sundown and he ain't never going to win the
Kentucky Derby."
—CARDINALS STAR PEPPER MARTIN, DISDAINING
TWICE-DAILY PRACTICES

● ● ●

"I'd rather be the Yankees catcher than the president and that makes me pretty lucky, I guess, because I could never be the president."
—YOGI BERRA, CATCHER

• • •

"Even Napoleon had his Watergate."
—PHILLIES MANAGER DANNY OZARK

• • •

"Does that mean I have to play Hamlet?"
—YANKEES SOUTHPAW RON GUIDRY, WHEN TOLD HE WOULD FILL SEVERAL ROLES FOR THE UPCOMING SEASON

• • •

"In ten years, Ed Kranepool has a chance to be a star. In ten years, Greg Goosen has a chance to be thirty."
—METS MANAGER CASEY STENGEL, WHEN ASKED ABOUT TWO TWENTY-YEAR-OLD PROSPECTS ON HIS ROSTER

• • •

"Our phenoms aren't phenomenating."
—CALIFORNIA ANGELS MANAGER LEFTY PHILLIPS

• • •

"Don't eat fried food, it angries up the blood."
—PITCHER SATCHEL PAIGE

• • •

"The other teams could make trouble for us if they win."
—YANKEES MANAGER YOGI BERRA

• • •

"It's youth, but that youth thing gets old after a while."
—PITCHING COACH DICK POLE ON A ROOKIE
HURLER

• • •

"Root only for the winner. That way you won't be disappointed."
—RELIEVER TUG MCGRAW

• • •

"They had better defense at Pearl Harbor."
—OUTFIELDER ANDY VAN SLYKE, DERIDING HIS
PIRATES TEAM DEFENSE

• • •

"The good Lord was good to me. He gave me a strong body, a
good right arm, and a weak mind."
—PITCHING GREAT DIZZY DEAN

• • •

"He's the best twenty-three-year-old catcher I've seen since Campy [Roy Campanella]—and Campy was twenty five years old the first time I saw him."
—MANAGER CASEY STENGEL ON JOHNNY BENCH

• • •

"If a guy is a good fastball hitter, does that mean I should throw him a bad fastball?"
—RELIEF PITCHER LARRY ANDERSEN

• • •

"It must be about an elbow specialist."
—PITCHER STEVE STONE WHEN HE SAW ORIOLES TEAMMATE JIM PALMER READING *DR. ZHIVAGO*

• • •

"I don't know. I never smoked Astroturf."
—RELIEVER TUG MCGRAW, WHEN ASKED IF HE PREFERS NATURAL GRASS OR ASTROTURF

• • •

"It's déjà vu all over again."
—CATCHER YOGI BERRA

• • •

"Let him hit ya'—I'll get you a new neck."
—CASEY STENGEL, METS MANAGER, TO HIS PLAYER
IN A BASES LOADED SITUATION

• • •

"I'd walk through hell in a gasoline suit to play baseball."
—REDS LEGEND PETE ROSE

• • •

"The Angels are the first team I've ever been on where I feel I
belong. They're all nuts, too."
—OUTFIELDER AND FORMER MENTAL PATIENT
JIMMY PIERSALL

• • •

"He said he broke it in two places; I, of course, told him to stay
out of those two places."
—PITCHER STEVE STONE ON JOSE RIJO'S BROKEN
ANKLE

• • •

"His reputations preceded him before he got here."
—YANKEES DON MATTINGLY ON METS HURLER
DWIGHT GOODEN

• • •

"He is dead at the present time."
—MANAGER CASEY STENGEL, REFERRING TO A
FORMER COLLEAGUE

• • •

"I asked the doctor before he closed the [head] wound if he could
put some brains in there."
—UTILITY PLAYER REX HUDLER

• • •

"I've seen the future and it's much like the present, only longer."
—ACE ROYALS RELIEVER DAN QUISENBERRY

• • •

"I'm not blind to hearing what everybody else hears."
—PITCHER ZANE SMITH ON SPECULATION HE
WOULD NOT BE KEPT ON BOSTON'S POSTSEASON
ROSTER

• • •

"There's no way they can bury twelve people out there."
—CATCHER BOB KEARNEY OF THE TWELVE
MONUMENTS IN CENTERFIELD AT YANKEE
STADIUM

• • •

"If anybody plays harder than Pete Rose, he's gotta be an outpatient."
—PHILLIES PITCHER TUG MCGRAW

• • •

"What is a captain supposed to do—go out on the field before the game and decide whether to kick or receive?"
—YANKEES CAPTAIN GRAIG NETTLES

• • •

"I'm looking forward to putting on my glasses with the fake nose so I can walk around and be a normal person."
—PITCHER DAN QUISENBERRY ON HIS PLANS FOR WHAT TO DO AFTER THE WORLD SERIES WAS OVER

• • •

"Does this mean I have to shave my legs?"
—OUTFIELDER ANDY VAN SLYKE, WHEN TOLD HIS TEAM HAD A POLICY OF NO HAIR BELOW THE LIP

• • •

"Thirty-two pounds per square inch at sea level."
—BOSTON PITCHER BILL "SPACEMAN" LEE WHEN, IN THE MIDST OF A TIGHT PENNANT RACE, HE WAS ASKED HOW MUCH PRESSURE HE WAS FEELING

• • •

"The world will end before there's another .400 hitter. I think that was mentioned in the Bible."
—PHILLIES STAR LENNY DYKSTRA

• • •

"When Charlie Finley had his heart operation, it took eight hours—seven just to find his heart."
—A'S PITCHER STEVE MCCATTY ON HIS TEAM'S OWNER

• • •

"There's one record I hold: Most World Series on the most different teams for a right-handed third baseman who didn't switch hit and who never played for the Yankees."
—HEINIE GROH, SIXTEEN-YEAR BIG LEAGUE VETERAN

• • •

"We've got a problem. Luis Tiant wants to use the bathroom and it says no foreign objects in the toilet."
—YANKEES GRAIG NETTLES WHILE ON A TEAM FLIGHT

• • •

"Kids should practice autographing baseballs. This is a skill that's often overlooked in Little League."
—PITCHER TUG MCGRAW

• • •

"I'd say he's done more than that."
—MANAGER YOGI BERRA, WHEN ASKED IF A
PLAYER HAD EXCEEDED HIS EXPECTATIONS

• • •

"We used to pray the White Sox and the Cubs would merge so
Chicago would have only one bad team."
—COMEDIAN TOM DREESEN, NATIVE OF CHICAGO

• • •

"They [pitchers] shouldn't throw at me—I'm the father of five or
six kids."
—INFIELDER TITO FUENTES

• • •

"I didn't think I was that bad a ballplayer, but they're making a
believer out of me."
—OUTFIELDER JIM GOSGER

• • •

"You have two hemispheres in your brain—a left and a right side.
The left side controls the right side of your body and the right
controls the left half. It's a fact. Therefore, left-handed pitchers are
the only people in their right minds."
—SOUTHPAW BILL LEE

• • •

"Sure I eat what I advertise. Sure I eat Wheaties for breakfast. A good bowl of Wheaties with bourbon can't be beat."
—PITCHER DIZZY DEAN

• • •

"I'm in the twilight of a mediocre career."
—FRANK SULLIVAN, RED SOX PITCHER

• • •

"A manager uses a relief pitcher like a six-shooter. He fires until it's empty and then takes the gun and throws it at the villain."
—RELIEVER DAN QUISENBERRY

• • •

"I'm going to play with harder nonchalance this year."
—BALTIMORE'S JACKIE BRANDT

• • •

"Damn, if this plane goes down I hope the newspapers at least have me listed in the probable starting pitches."
—PITCHER JIM BOUTON DURING A ROUGH FLIGHT

• • •

"I don't think it will affect his mobility. Electrical storms might be a problem."
—CATCHER JIM TORBORG ON A METAL PLATE SURGICALLY PLACED IN CARLTON FISK'S THROWING ARM

● ● ●

"That way I can see where I've been. I always know where I'm going."
—OUTFIELDER JIMMY PIERSALL ON RUNNING THE BASES BACKWARD UPON HITTING HIS HUNDREDTH HOME RUN

● ● ●

"When I was young and smart, I couldn't understand Casey Stengel. Now that I'm older and dumber, he makes sense to me."
—DODGERS GREAT SANDY KOUFAX

● ● ●

"It gets late early out there."
—HALL OF FAMER YOGI BERRA ON THE DIFFICULTY OF PLAYING IN THE SHADOWS OF LEFT FIELD IN YANKEE STADIUM

● ● ●

"A few million years from now the sun will burn out and lose its gravitational pull. The earth will turn into a giant snowball and be hurled through space. When that happens, it won't matter if I get this guy out."
—PITCHER BILL LEE

• • •

"Fractured, hell. The damn thing's broken."
—HALL OF FAME PITCHER DIZZY DEAN, WHEN TOLD BY A DOCTOR THAT HIS TOE WAS FRACTURED

• • •

"All I'm asking for is what I want."
—STOLEN BASE KING RICKEY HENDERSON ON HIS MONEY DEMANDS DURING HIS CONTRACT NEGOTIATIONS

• • •

"You give 100 percent in the first half of the game and if that isn't enough, in the second half you give what's left."
—YOGI BERRA AS A YANKEES COACH

• • •

"A lot of relief pitchers develop a crazy facade and it's this facade that helps them deal with the pressure. Of course, maybe it's only the crazies that want to be relief pitchers."
—RELIEVER SKIP LOCKWOOD

• • •

"If you act like you know what you're doing, you can do anything you want—except maybe perform neural surgery."
—OUTFIELDER JOHN LOWENSTEIN

• • •

"Most of the time, I don't even know what I said until I read about it. But I really didn't say everything I said."
—YANKEES YOGI BERRA

• • •

"He's missing something upstairs, but that's what makes him a player."
—UTILITY PLAYER TONY PHILLIPS ON ANGELS TEAMMATE REX HUDLER

• • •

"A lot of people who don't say 'ain't' ain't eating."
—DIZZY DEAN, WHEN CRITICIZED FOR USING THE WORD "AIN'T" ON THE AIR

• • •

"There comes a time in every man's life—and I've had plenty of them."
—COLORFUL MANAGER CASEY STENGEL

• • •

"What can you expect in a 'northpaw' world?"
—LEFTY RELIEVER BILL LEE, WHEN ASKED WHY LEFTIES ARE SUCH FLAKES

• • •

"Sure, I screwed up that sacrifice bunt, but look at it this way: I'm a better bunter than a billion Chinese."
—ORIOLES JOHN LOWENSTEIN

• • •

"I got good stamina, I got good wind, and the heat ain't got me, but I just don't have a good fastball."
—DODGERS PITCHER PREACHER ROE

• • •

"You don't get your first home run too often."
—CATCHER RICK WRONA ON HIS FIRST BIG LEAGUE BLAST

• • •

"Teaching baseball to five-year-olds is like trying to organize a bunch of earthworms."
—WRITER DOROTHY C. MCCONNELL

• • •

"This winter I'm working out every day, throwing at a wall. I'm 11 and 0 against the wall."
—PITCHER JIM BOUTON

• • •

"I guess I'd better send my fingers to Cooperstown."
—PITCHER DENNIS LAMP, AFTER LOU BROCK'S HISTORIC THREE-THOUSANDTH HIT CAME ON A BALL WHICH DEFLECTED OFF LAMP'S HAND

• • •

"If I knew I was going to live this long, I'd have taken better care of myself."
—YANKEE STAR MICKEY MANTLE, TURNING FORTY-SIX, BUT ALSO CREDITED TO UMPIRE CAL HUBBARD

• • •

"If he played for me, I wouldn't handle him with a strong arm; I'd handle him with a straightjacket like the rest of the nuts."
—MANAGER BILLY MARTIN ON THE FLAKY BILL LEE

• • •

"It would be an honor to get something like that—I have lots of trophies at home, but I bought them myself."
—PITCHER BERT BLYLEVEN ON HIS THOUGHTS ABOUT POSSIBLY WINNING THE COMEBACK PLAYER OF THE YEAR AWARD

PART TWELVE

• • •

The Beauty, Joy, and Love of Baseball

Baseball prose often takes on qualities of poetry. Words flow from pens and off tongues as smoothly and as ornately as icing being squeezed atop a wedding cake.

Many of us who love the game argue that baseball is a sport unlike any other in that it is so powerfully evocative. Gloomy domes and a few other unimaginative cookie cutter ballparks and bleak facilities such as the Oakland "Mausoleum" aside, even baseball's playing venues have given birth to eternal words of awe; baseball fans and writers alike gush over the beauty of a Camden Yards and a PNC Park of today and display schoolboy nostalgia over the glory of Ebbets and Forbes Fields.

Baseball has spawned volumes of observations which often have good intentions yet are rife with, or border on, mushy sentimentality. Meanwhile, other copious comments on the beauty, joy, and love of the game are downright beautiful in themselves. Both have their place.

Not only that, but those who have penned or spoken those countless words are not just players with a vested interest in the game and members of the media, those assigned to and therefore obligated to pound out words by the truckload for the companies that purchase ink by the barrel. No, baseball is a topic which has attracted the heavy hitters, the sluggers of the literati, as well. How's this for a roll call: Mark Twain, Robert Frost, Walt Whitman, George Will, and David Halberstam, all included in this chapter.

Further, writers in any field don't come much better than, say, Roger Angell, Thomas Boswell, Jim Murray, Red Smith, and Roger Kahn, sportswriters and true devotees of baseball. In the following pages, the men who expounded on the joy of baseball also include President Franklin D. Roosevelt, famed attorney Clarence Darrow, and General Douglas MacArthur.

Plus, it never hurts to take in the words of those who have lived the game, men such as colorful, maverick team owner Bill Veeck, whose love of baseball was deep, and players such as Nolan Ryan and Tom Seaver.

They're all here, professing their love of baseball and marveling at the joy and the beauty of the game.

● ● ●

"Every day was Mardi Gras and every fan a king."
—CLEVELAND BASEBALL OWNER BILL VEECK ON
HOW HE TREATED HIS FANS, FROM *VEECK AS IN
WRECK*

• • •

"The strongest thing baseball has going for it today is
yesterdays."
—SPORTSWRITER LAWRENCE S. RITTER, FROM *THE
GLORY OF THEIR TIMES*

• • •

"Dream into the open spaces of the baseball turf, even if you're
not there at the park. You're there anyway."
—WRITER MARVIN COHEN

• • •

"A hot dog at the ballpark is better than steak at the Ritz."
—ACTOR HUMPHREY BOGART

• • •

"I'll be looking at how many years in a row I was able to go out
there and be consistent. Not because it was about the dollars or
it was about the publicity or whatever, but because the game was
meant to be played a certain way."
—SLUGGER MO VAUGHN ON HOW HE'D LOOK BACK
AT HIS CAREER AFTER RETIRING, FROM *BASEBALL
DIGEST,* SEPTEMBER 1998

• • •

"The game will survive long past you or I."
—TEAM OWNER BILL VEECK

• • •

"Correct thinkers think that 'baseball trivia' is an oxymoron:
nothing about baseball is trivial."
—WRITER GEORGE F. WILL

• • •

"Baseball is simple, but never easy."
—SPORTSWRITER ROGER ANGELL

• • •

"Next to religion, baseball has had a greater impact on the
American people than any other institution."
—UNITED STATES PRESIDENT HERBERT HOOVER

• • •

"I love the tradition and I love the drama. Every baseball game
has drama. It's not just an end-of-the-season thing. I love the
pace. I mean, it just works. All the way through."
—FORMER BASEBALL COMMISSIONER PETER
UEBERROTH

• • •

"I didn't even graduate from high school. I ate and slept baseball all my life."
—PITCHER SMOKY JOE WOOD ON HIS LOVE AND DEDICATION TO THE GAME

• • •

"Baseball is not a life-or-death situation and in the big picture, this game is just a small part of our lives. The important thing is to use baseball to help other people."
—SUPERSTAR KEN GRIFFEY, JR.

• • •

"Baseball is one of the arts."
—BOSTON'S TED WILLIAMS

• • •

"You may glory in a team triumphant, but you fall in love with a team in defeat."
—WRITER ROGER KAHN

• • •

"Baseball gives every American boy a chance to excel, not just to be as good as someone else but to be better than someone else. That is the nature of man and the name of the game."
—HALL OF FAMER TED WILLIAMS

• • •

"Spring is a time of year when the ground thaws, trees bud, the income tax falls due—and everybody wins the pennant."
—WRITER JIM MURRAY

• • •

"Give a boy a bat and a ball and a place to play and you'll have a good citizen."
—HALL OF FAMER JOE MCCARTHY

• • •

"I always wonder if the fans are seeing enough. If you stay with this game and really watch it, your appreciation goes much deeper. It rewards you."
—CATCHER TED SIMMONS

• • •

"Good players feel the kind of love for the game that they did when they were Little Leaguers."
—HALL OF FAME PITCHER TOM SEAVER

• • •

"You should enter a ballpark the way you enter a church."
—PITCHER BILL LEE

• • •

"The clock doesn't matter in baseball. Time stands still or moves backward. Theoretically, one game could go on forever. . . ."
—HERB CAEN, WRITER FOR THE *SAN FRANCISCO CHRONICLE*

• • •

"Baseball is the very symbol, the outward and visible expression of the drive and push and rush and struggle of the raging, tearing, booming nineteenth century."
—AUTHOR MARK TWAIN

• • •

"When a poor American boy dreamed of escaping his grim life, his fantasy probably involved becoming a professional baseball player. It was not so much the national sport as the binding national myth."
—WRITER DAVID HALBERSTAM

• • •

"Baseball is the fabric of the American soul. The cliché goes: Baseball is as American as apple pie. I say more so. You can buy apple pie anywhere, but baseball is still a kid and his father shagging fly balls on a June afternoon at the park."
—LARRY KING, TELEVISION HOST, FROM *WHAT BASEBALL MEANS TO ME*

• • •

"The only perfect pleasure we ever knew."
—FAMOUS ATTORNEY CLARENCE DARROW ON HIS
YOUTH AND BASEBALL

• • •

"It's fun, it's timeless, it's a relationship between a father and a
son, it's a transition into manhood."
—PITCHER BILL LEE

• • •

"If you're not having fun in baseball, you miss the point of
everything."
—FIRST BASEMAN CHRIS CHAMBLISS

• • •

"One of the beautiful things about baseball is that every once in
a while you come into a situation where you want to, and where
you have to, reach down and prove something."
—PITCHING GREAT NOLAN RYAN

• • •

"More than any other American sport, baseball creates the mag-
netic, addictive illusion that it can almost be understood."
—SPORTSWRITER THOMAS BOSWELL

• • •

"Baseball is a ballet without music. Drama without words. A carnival without kewpie dolls. Baseball is continuity. Pitch to pitch. Inning to inning. Season to season."
—TIGERS BROADCASTER ERNIE HARWELL, FROM *BASEBALL AND THE MEANING OF LIFE,* EDITED BY JOSH LEVENTHAL

• • •

"Baseball is a sport dominated by vital ghosts; it's a fraternity, like no other we have of the active and the no longer so, the living and the dead."
—WRITER RICHARD GILMAN

• • •

"For some of us, there is a peculiar attraction to baseball. It has its own drama. I have always loved the game. I don't care whether or not it's childish."
—AUTHOR JAMES T. FARRELL

• • •

"Any baseball is beautiful. No other small package comes as close to the ideal in design and utility. It is a perfect object for a man's hand. Pick it up and it instantly suggests its purpose: It is meant to be thrown a considerable distance—thrown hard and with precision."
—SPORTSWRITER ROGER ANGELL, FROM *FIVE SEASONS*

• • •

"No game in the world is as tidy and dramatically neat as baseball, with cause and effect, crime and punishment, motive and result so cleanly defined."
—SPORTSWRITER PAUL GALLICO

• • •

"Baseball is almost the only orderly thing in a very unorderly world. If you get three strikes, even the best lawyer in the world can't get you off."
—TEAM OWNER BILL VEECK

• • •

"It also makes it easy for the generations to talk to one another."
—POET JOEL OPPENHEIMER ON THE JOYS OF BASEBALL

• • •

"What seems apparent to me is that close analysis is pointless. The game is there. It is the best game there is. That's all I need to know."
—ART HILL, SPORTSWRITER

• • •

Index

Index

Index

211